T0150163

WE NEED TO ACT

Other titles by Jonathan Jansen

Great South African Teachers
We Need to Talk
Oor Bokdrolletjies en Rosyntjies
Briewe Aan My Kinders
Letters to my Children

JONATHAN JANSEN

WE NEED TO ACT

© Jonathan Jansen 2013

All rights reserved. No part of this book may be reproduced or transmitted in any form or by any means, electronic or mechanical, including photocopying, recording or any information storage or retrieval system, without permission from the copyright holder.

ISBN 978-1-920434-58-8

First edition, first impression 2013

Published jointly by
Bookstorm (Pty) Ltd and Pan Macmillan South Africa (Pty) Ltd

PO Box 4532	Private Bag X19
Northcliff 2115	Northlands 2116
Johannesburg	Johannesburg
South Africa	South Africa
www.bookstorm.co.za	**www.panmacmillan.co.za**

Distributed by Pan Macmillan
via Booksite Afrika

Edited by Wesley Thompson
Proofread by John Henderson
Cover design by Triple M Design
Typeset by Lebone Publishing Services
Printed by Ultra Litho (Pty) Ltd, Johannesburg

ACKNOWLEDGEMENTS

This is something I always look forward to – acknowledging the many tributaries of ideas, inspiration and sheer good luck that come together in a single stream of columns of 750 words each, due every Wednesday by 12h00 or else Carolyn Fish at *The Times* will send you that gentle reminder as the deadline approaches. Carolyn always signs off, week after week, with a varied word of thanks for the column just sent and sometimes a word of encouragement. Thank you, Carolyn, for managing the time of a busy writer.

I should thank my ruthless early-morning and late-night editor, my wife, Grace, for her willingness to read rough drafts of the various columns and give direct and critical comments about whether the narrative thread holds and whether it 'connects' with the reader. I often disagree out of irritation, but make the changes anyway, with astounding results.

There is no better book publisher on this planet than the understated Louise Grantham of Bookstorm. I am astounded at how Louise anticipates an audience, 'sees' connections and disconnections across columns and chapters, and articulates the strengths and weaknesses of writing so well. With her outstanding team of colleagues in design, marketing and editing – including the team from Pan Macmillan, I actually do very little other than put pen to paper. Basil van Rooyen remains the wise old man who shares my love of Afrikaans as a tool for getting to the bottom of things in unflattering terms.

Then I must thank the people I underestimate. The old man who put petrol into my car in Beaufort West and right at the end of the routine, as I took the slip, told me: 'I follow your writings since your BC days; it got better.' I thank the *Bergie* (beggar) at the Wembley Roadhouse in Athlone, Cape Town, who stood in the rain as he knocked on the window of my car until I rolled down it down in frustration: 'I read your column in *The Times* every Thursday.' And my gratitude to the newspaper guy at the Pretoria robots who refused to move from the front of my car until I acknowledged him as a regular reader. And to all the South Africans who read the column and say nice things about waiting for Thursdays, thank you. What you say means a lot to me and I really hope this collection makes it easier to access, retain and mull over the ideas about a country which still has so much potential to live up to those Mandela values which we all so admire, often from a distance.

I thank those politicians and government officials who, I am told, regularly read the Thursday column with varying measures of anxiety. Surely you have better things to do? More seriously, I trust you sense in all these offerings a deep loyalty to our country. One of you, a cabinet minister, asked a mutual friend: 'Who is this man? Where is he coming from?' I can answer that by drawing on a powerful quote from another of my heroes, Martin Luther King Jr, the American civil rights leader, who said this to the annoyance of his government for resisting US policies abroad: 'I am against the war in Vietnam because I love America.'

And, finally, I thank my more than 33 000 students at the University of the Free State. You continue to inspire me with your ability to defy history, to overcome division, and to show South Africa and the world that there is another way of dealing with bitterness and injustice. I write, for you.

CONTENTS

WE NEED TO ACT FOR THE FUTURE

WE NEED TO ACT FOR SERVICE DELIVERY

WE NEED TO ACT IN HOPE

EPILOGUE 294

INTRODUCTION: A CASE FOR CITIZEN ACTION

A feline dilemma

Stray cats. Of all the student requests, complaints or demands (the choice of approach often depends on how the student was raised) that flood my Facebook and Twitter accounts in any given week, stray cats could not possibly be a priority for a university principal. Yet there was something intriguing in the student's plea; not only was this a 'first' on my desk in many years in education, but the resolution of the problem was shocking, to say the least.

The young woman was burdened by the sheer number of stray cats roaming on campus. So this animal biology student did something about the problem: she caught the campus cats and sterilised them. But she cannot keep up with the scale of the problem, so she seeks my assistance to figure out how we could tackle this problem of stray cats, together.

I find this story exciting for several reasons. To begin with, in my four years on campus I do not recall seeing cats, maybe one or two, here and there, sometimes. I think this is the problem with social change and why so few citizens come to act on problems of literacy or poverty or childcare. It takes a special person to actually 'see' these problems in the everyday where many of us are so accustomed to the challenges around us that they become invisible; try to remember how many beggars you passed on the street and at the robots on your way home. See?

Then there is the felt burden, the deep concern that touches the heart of this student. There is angst in the Facebook posting, an urgency she wants to convey. For other student activists it is hungry students or learners without textbooks. What frames her social concern as an individual is stray cats.

The student then decides to do something about the problem. In doing so she draws on her own skills as a biologist and finds sterilisation equipment somewhere. Sterilising the cats will put an end to the scores of hungry, scavenging animals roaming the campus. And it is only after taking action herself that the student seeks to build a broader network of supporters to get behind her idea.

I can hear somebody raising questions of the legality of the action and it is quite likely that the SPCA might be calling for names and numbers which, of course, I will refuse to give them. But this is social action at its very best: it disturbs common sense with uncommon valour. It does not wait for official action to emerge, if at all. This social activist draws on her own resources to make the change happen.

Why government cannot do it alone (or at all)

As I travel up and down South Africa I meet so many people like my animal biology student. I meet grandmothers who, without being asked, gather pre-school children playing on the streets and teach them songs and skills and values in a backyard or a shack. I know high school students who approached their principal to offer support to communities ravaged by the ugliness of xenophobia. I see how university students, on their own steam, go into township schools on weekends offering extra maths, science and accounting lessons – expecting nothing in return.

These activists all share one thing in common: they do not wait for government to act. When the textbooks did not reach the poorest schools of Limpopo province, I lost count of how many companies, non-governmental organisations and individuals offered to deliver the textbooks. But pride is a terrible thing; our government refused help (and not only from rival political parties with their own grandstanding agendas, of course).

Even the most cautious South African leader, scared of criticism and worse, will tell you – often in whispered tones as if someone might overhear – that our government simply does not have the capacity, the commitment or the competence in many fields of social services to deliver what our people need. It is very clear to me as a student of policy that *systemic change* is not going to happen for a very long time, and certainly not (to coin a useless phrase) in our lifetime.

This does not mean there will not be impressive documents like the National Development Plan. It does not mean, further, that local and national politicians will not boast about how many billions they pled in the budget for their portfolio – this should be a point of embarrassment, not pride, since such high levels of resource should translate into results. In education alone, that is not happening. Nor does it mean that ahead of an election year politicians will not be seen handing out keys to new homeowners waiting for years on those interminable lists. But this is not systemic change; it is symbolic change which mainly serves narrow political interests, ministerial image and opportunistic deflection from the real problems we simply cannot change.

Like all nationalist governments, our rulers place comradeship above competence. This does not mean that there are not competent comrades; when pressed on this matter the comrades correctly mention Pravin Gordhan or Trevor Manuel or Naledi Pandor or Aaron Motsoaledi as competent and selfless leaders from within the ranks of the ruling party. Up and down the civil service I have been privileged to meet highly competent individuals, a prime example being Dr Cassius Lubisi, Director General in the President's Office; this decent man is also a specialist in mathematics education and a good friend – though he no longer returns my calls, for some reason. But these are a minority: most of the comrades serving are incompetent and hold their positions for no other reason than loyalty to the party or, as regimes change, loyalty to a particular set of leaders in the party at one time.

Take a good look at the municipalities of poor areas – like Kroonstad in the Free State – and you will bear witness to two of the great evils of our time, incompetence and corruption. Take a look at serial offenders in the cabinet exposed time after time for the wastage of taxpayers' monies or the inability to deliver basic materials to schools, and you will see why government cannot and will not be able to serve all its people with the resources at its disposal.

But there is another reason why government fails to reach all citizens through its mandate to govern. It continues to impose racial preferences on employment. Some of this I understand, such as the decision to hire black cadets for training as future pilots. But why hire only black cadets? Why do exactly what the white nationalists did – hire only white cadets? Why not hire 80% black cadets and continue to bring in the most competent white cadets as well? What a powerful message this will send, of seeking only the best while at the same time correcting, through numbers, the injustice of having mainly white male pilots in the system?

The problem we face is that our government, in failing to draw on the full range of talented and competent people available to rebuild this country, does exactly the opposite; it holds back the reliable delivery of opportunities and services for those at the lower end of the social, economic and educational pyramid.

We can of course sit back and criticise government for excluding competent people from the talent pool that can be mobilised to serve; or we can do it ourselves.

The return of the activist citizen
In a relatively short period of time there has been a mushrooming of citizen initiatives of all kinds to start doing something independent of government or, in some cases, with government leaders on invitational terms. Think of the powerful role of an NGO like Equal Education and how it has mobilised prominent South African leaders to publicise the horrific state of schools in the Eastern Cape; or how it has become that little stone in the shoes of gov-

ernment by repeated appeals to the courts to force commitments from officialdom on textbook deliveries in rural areas or set norms for the provision of infrastructure.

Before Mamphela Ramphele turned her citizen's movement into a political party, she led a powerful coalition of influential people to leave their jobs and become part of a broad strategy to change education. Bobby Godsell, the mining intellectual (never thought those two words could come together) and James Motlatsi, the founding Secretary General of the National Union of Mineworkers, also launched a Citizen's Movement that brings together leading lights from across society to make public commitments to change in South Africa.

I write this introduction on a plane returning from New York where I had the privilege of addressing more than 200 people, many of them activists from the anti-apartheid movement, who have now turned their energies into an international citizen's movement for change under the tireless leadership of James Urdang and Dan Fisher and their group, Education Africa. As the auction and 'text your pledge' (you pledge money for South African education on your cell phone and it shows immediately on a big screen for all to read) got underway, I realised how ordinary Americans have come to form part of this broader movement of people to affect change in our country.

Gone are the days of complaining that development NGOs had to shut down because foreign embassies re-channelled their money to the new, democratic government of Nelson Mandela, leaving citizen initiative high and dry. I know that some international governments – as well as foundations and corporations – are beginning to re-think their strategy of a government-centric view of funding and beginning to ask how new monies can strengthen civil society in the face of what seems to be political inertia in redressing pressing social problems like education.

A self-interest claim for selflessness

This is the message of *We Need to Act*, a sequel of course to its predecessor, *We Need to Talk*. There are **at least seven reasons** why I believe that citizen action is vitally necessary as we come out of the heady days of post-apartheid euphoria.

One, if ordinary citizens do nothing we face the real problem of even greater social instability than some analysts already predict in the light of stubborn unemployment and intractable crises in the poorest schools. Think of the problem this way: in every cycle of 12 years of schooling, about half a million youths fail to make a successful transition from Grade 1 through Grade 12. Where do you think most of those youths went? They lurk in the dark, many of them engaged in rituals of addiction and violence, perpetrators of reckless crimes that destroy their own families and the families of those they do not know. Even if there is no compassion to serve these volatile youths for their own sake, an even selfish appeal should convince all of us that we stabilise whole communities by taking on the problem of social and educational dropouts.

Two, if we do nothing as active citizens, we become part of the narrative of hopelessness. In other words, by serving others we improve ourselves. We gain insight into social problems we might not be part of; those in good schools need to know about the state of schools that are failing, and with this understanding we all become more knowledgeable and better placed to make a difference. There is something sacred in service; by reaching out to help, we convey a sense of hope to server and served alike.

Three, if we do nothing to act on our problems we break the chain of a long history of activists over the centuries, people who in even more dire situations stood up to poverty and illiteracy, to violent government and dangerous gangs, and gave us this young democracy to work with. I like celebrating great turning points in history, like the Soweto-inspired uprisings of the youth in 1976; but the message from that rebellion is that we have real evidence from the past that ordinary people changed their own circumstances, over and over again.

Four, if we do nothing, millions of marginalised people are themselves doomed. There are problems so complex and distant from governmental action that only citizens in the small corners of the country, its towns and townships, can ever penetrate with action that transforms and empowers fellow human beings. Think of how many young people are shot and killed in drive-by shootings in the cyclical gang wars of the Cape Flats. Think of the endless parade of black male bodies lying on the streets after another intercepted gang heist. Think of how drugs have fuelled rape and murder across the cities and townships of this country. And then ask yourself whether courts and prisons alone can stop this relentless march to the grave of unreached potential among young people.

Five, if we do nothing we fail to demonstrate to the next generation how to live their lives. Our children become like us through observation. The miscreants throwing human waste onto the steps of the Western Cape legislature and onto the shiny floors of Cape Town International Airport have learnt from the elders the politics of insult and disgust – that the way to behave in public is to bring out the worst in human endeavour. Children who see parents live selfish lives consumed by material pursuit will in most cases themselves look down on the helping professions such as teaching or nursing or social work; their preoccupation is more likely to be the kinds of qualifications that rake in the money. We extend the chain of generosity into the next generation through lives that demonstrate duty and service.

Six, we serve in order to compensate for things we did wrong in the past. I will never forget the day one of my colleagues, a mild-mannered man called Peet Venter, interrupted my talk to about five white teachers and principals who were retired from active teaching, and who decided to join my team that set the simple goal of improving teaching and learning in the most disadvantaged schools of the Free State province. 'Thank you,' he said, 'for the opportunity to work on this project. It is the only way we can give back and make up for what we as white people did wrong in the past.' I was stunned; that came out of nowhere. But it made sense. I am sure Dr Peet, as we call him, did not hurt a soul in the past and I know he lives off a modest salary without many material possessions. But Dr Peet sees service as a way of dealing with his own demons and making his relative advantage work in the interests of black children.

Seven, we serve because it is within the logic of our upbringing to 'plough back', as my late mother often put it, once you have been able to move ahead. I love the stories of business leaders or civil servants or well-employed individuals going back to the communities that raised them to lend a helping hand. For those of us from very poor families, it is a common story that one of the children was sent to work to enable the older or smarter sibling to continue schooling. The education of so many of our people is a community affair; ask students at university graduation ceremonies how many of them studied with the help of the pension of a grandmother or a loan from a neighbour or a contribution from an uncle. The logic is persuasive, therefore, that if you got ahead through the help of others, go back and help others to succeed. There is something profoundly moving about this circle of service within communities.

Conclusion

I thank the poor student who came to see me during one of those early morning 'open door' sessions on campus. She was so proud of the fact that she had given a gift to her classmate, a wheelchair. The young woman took my hand and led me to the waiting room outside my office where I saw her beaming student friend in his shiny new possession that made it possible for him to attend classes. In any country, this would be a moving story of activism to make a difference, where you are. But what are the chances, anywhere, of a poor student raising funds and emptying her own pockets for a poor classmate? Then, wait for it. What are the chances of a poor white student doing this for a poor black student in a country where racial indifference and racial intolerance still mark our post-apartheid landscape? That single event transformed me deeply, and reaffirmed my faith in the capacity of giving to bridge both psychological and material divides.

When I wrote the story of Nozimanga Bonje, the primary school girl who was raped by a relative the one year, only to witness in a following year her beloved mother slain at the hands of her father, South Africans emptied their pockets to enable this strong young woman to pursue university studies. She had to clean the floor herself where her mother's blood lay splattered across the floor. Yet Nozi, as she likes to be called, emerged strong and confident from this unspeakable ordeal. What I will never forget was the old woman from Durban who called and told me that after she had paid the people she owed, she had only R20 left. Do I think that would be enough to help Nozi? I choked up, of course, and said that 20 cents would be enough to add to the generous givers that so much wanted Nozi to succeed.

Every month without fail there are still active citizens who pay over R1 000 to R5 000 and more into a dedicated university account to ensure that Nozi gets her degree. We are now also able to support other poor students with compelling human stories and exceptional academic results.

I want to thank every one of you for giving in such a generous and consistent way to transform not only one life but a family's life and, if Nozi gets her way, the life of a whole community. Nozi applied to medical school but decided to first do a Bachelor of Science degree in Human Molecular Biology before reapplying to do medicine. She passed all her first-semester modules with exceptional results in some subjects – and this despite receiving most of her education in very disadvantaged schools before completing her senior years at Eunice Girls' School. It was this broad base of support for Nozi from across colours and classes, and from all parts of the country, that made me realise, again, that given a chance, South Africans will support hope wherever we find it.

In many ways the stories contained in *We Need to Act* are stories about giving. It is about giving up our selfish ways so that self-interest yields to the interests of others. It is about giving away what we have whether in abundance or in short supply. It is about giving to redeem ourselves and others. It is about giving to preserve ourselves, the lowest motivation for the giver. It is, in the final analysis, about giving that keeps alive among all of us the possibility of living out the hope an ageing 94-year-old left as a sacred gift when he emerged from a long and unjust prison sentence.

It is to that man, who gave of himself for total strangers, that I dedicate this book.

WE NEED TO ACT
FOR EDUCATION

*'What we cannot do is relive this stress and
tension year after year in the lives of poor
students and vulnerable institutions.'*

Good intentions go wobbly

Build our nation in forgotten schools

27 April 2011

Greenacres High (not its real name) used to be one of the most reputable public schools in South Africa. It was a former Model C school in a white working- to lower-middle-class area.

The parents worked hard for their money, and invested their time and limited resources to ensure that the school retained good teachers and a strong learning culture. When the 1990s came, the parents did the right thing – they opened the school to black children from as far away as the large township on the outskirts of the city.

Since then, the school has been proud to maintain, for more than a decade, a strong academic reputation and a disciplined learning environment.

It even won an award from a previous minister of education as one of the 'best integrated schools' in the country.

The parents contributed liberally to a special bursary fund to support poor black pupils who could not afford even the modest school fees that applied.

Then things went sour. There was more and more pressure from the government's district office to take in more and more children from the townships. The school tried to explain that the governing body did not want more than 25 children per classroom because larger numbers make classroom management more difficult and individual learning attention impossible.

The district official would hear none of this, hinting strongly that any resistance to his will would mean the school was 'racist'.

In the meantime, poor parents, long dissatisfied with the horrible conditions of township schooling, heard that Greenacres was one of those schools where it was easy to enrol their children.

Highly disruptive children unofficially blacklisted in the township schools also found their way to Greenacres, where at least they could secure a place.

When the governing body made the case that it wanted to give first preference to children from their catchment area, and later to at least half the children from the residences around the school, a group of disgruntled black parents organised a placard demonstration outside the school with the unflattering message: 'Greenacres is racist'. The district official joined the demonstration.

In a little while, the white parents left, deeply concerned about growing classes of more than 30 pupils, disgruntled by the regular external political threats to the school and the labelling of parents as racist, and distraught by the growing incidence of violence on the school premises – three stabbings in as many months.

As the race and class base of the school shifted to a poor, all-black school, there was no more money to fund extra teachers, arrange learning excursions or sustain a sports and music programme at the school. Worse, the school was still funded and treated by the provincial department of education as if it were a privileged white school.

No, I did not make this up. I know of many schools like Greenacres, and one such school was the subject of a scholarly book I researched and co-authored, *Diversity High: Class, Colour, Culture, and Character in a South African High School.*

Since the publication of the book, I have heard stories almost daily of schools such as Greenacres.

I call them wobbly schools.

There are at the moment in South Africa three types of school.

Type one is the strong minority of former white public and private schools, which strongly regulate admissions, maintain good academic results and retain a rich balance of racial diversity in the student body.

Type two is the large majority of poor township schools, all-black, which we read about daily as dysfunctional schools.

Sandwiched between these two types are the wobbly schools. Wobbly schools are being transformed from type one into type two schools daily, so spreading the rot of dysfunctionality in education.

As working-class white schools, they are more vulnerable to political pressure and financial hardship than their more affluent type one counterparts, which can trot out super lawyers from among the parents to challenge the government.

Type one schools are left alone by the new elite in the government, for this is where the black elites send their own children – and we do not want to collapse them as well.

It is, furthermore, in the wobbly schools, with poorer white and black learners, that the project of nation building is more urgent than in the type one schools, where children learn to forge and feign exemplary racial manners.

Stop empty promises

More government funding is needed for poor students with good marks

21 February 2013

Nqobile Mdaka did something very risky for an 18-year-old girl who had never left home.

She left her township outside Nelspruit with a suitcase a few weeks ago and headed for a taxi rank. She boarded an unsteady taxi to Johannesburg, then another one to Bloemfontein.

She did not have a cent to her name. She landed in Bloemfontein and hoped to find, somewhere, the R70 000 needed to cover her accommodation in residence, tuition, textbooks, groceries and toiletries. All she had was the promise.

The eldest child of unemployed parents, she left behind siblings in school armed only with a Statement of Results from the National Senior Certificate which showed remarkably high results for a student from a seriously disadvantaged township school. She clutched that paper with good marks; this was the promise, that if she did well in school, she might just be able to study at university one day.

'Sign here,' said one of my secretaries. 'There is no more money left and registration has closed; the student has to go home. Sign so that we can at least pay the bus tickets back to Nelspruit.'

Emotionally, 2013 has been my toughest year yet when it comes to student finances. I am not sure whether it is because of the reckless public statements by politicians that no poor student will be denied study, or the promise that 2014 will be a 'fee-free' year for university.

Whatever the electoral motivations of heartless politicians, the students hear these messages and show up holding that paper. I can see it in their eyes: 'You made a promise in 1994; our leaders make promises every day; have you not heard the promises from Pretoria? We are here to claim that promise.'

If only our promises were real. Thousands of students are streaming home right now from South Africa's 23 universities because there is no money despite the promise.

I simply cannot bring down the pen to sign the paper, and ask to see the young woman.

'What is your name, dear student?'

With a delightful click of the tongue: 'Nqobile, sir.'

I ask her to tell me her story. She was found crying in her university residence by another student, a senior from Pretoria, who then called her mother, who in turn offered to pay the registration fees.

It is time to call the mother. Portia Matlala sounds depressed but there is some life in her voice when I call.

'I am driving,' she says, 'and my radio is even off; I am feeling so sad for that student who my daughter told me about.'

I read Matlala's email: 'I was willing to pay for her registration fee [R10 890] today so she can pursue her degree. I do not expect her to pay me back. I just wanted to give an opportunity to get a degree. Unfortunately, late this afternoon she was informed that even if I pay she will not be able to register because registration closed.'

I tell her not to worry, we will register and pay for the student, and she could perhaps contribute to the books. The relief in the voice of the stranger carries over the phone lines as the university and a parent strike up a partnership to support the Nelspruit teenager.

We need to sort out the national crisis in student financing as soon as possible. The best minds in the country need to be brought together to find a sustainable strategy for funding students in need. The National Student Financial Aid Scheme (NSFAS) does not have enough money to cover all students. Moving around existing university subsidy funds in favour of student loans and bursaries will simply collapse already fragile institutional infrastructures.

The answer might lie in fresh ideas from the private sector and creative ways of incentivising ordinary citizens to invest in a national bursary scheme beyond the instruments available. Ordinary citizens like Matlala, whose heart for a stranger will change not one but many lives in Nelspruit.

What we cannot do is relive this stress and tension year after year in the lives of poor students and vulnerable institutions. More than one university has already seen violent strikes as students, in their ignorance, turn on their universities when the problem lies with the limited capacity of NSFAS to fund all academically smart but financially poor students.

Something must be done, urgently, or the promise will mean nothing.

Testing times for kids

How much learning actually goes on inside South African schools and universities?

3 November 2011

I do not mean how many facts are memorised at short notice to regurgitate in the final exam. I mean learning, variously defined as a transformation in the meaning of a student's experience; the altering of beliefs; the changing of behaviour; the things we think we actually send our children to school for.

Sometimes seismic shifts in education take place without anyone noticing. It kind of sneaks up on you, so you take what happens in school and classroom life for granted. One of those shifts, I dare to say, has been the move away from a concern for learning to a preoccupation with testing.

The next time you have a child in school, simply tick off the number of times the child writes tests and examinations. In many high schools, early on teachers begin to focus on 'what is required' for the upcoming examinations; this obsession takes on feverish proportions as children move from Grade 10 to Grade 12.

To understand this obsession with writing tests you have to understand what propels the school system in this direction.

There is enormous pressure on students to do well in these often-mindless tests because of an often-misplaced interest in the children's future.

The smartest children pick up on the cue that doing well in academic subjects is good for them, and this draws praise from all quarters. So what did some of them do?

They took more than a dozen subjects. I remember a child at a Pretoria school who somehow got more than 20 distinctions in what was then called 'matric'. Such a child is not only a danger to society, but a danger to higher education. Can you imagine the kind of stress this child must have passed through to attain this ridiculous feat?

What does this say about the overall health of a child when obviously all the time available for living was consumed in this senseless game of impressing adults? When, in fact, did learning take place?

But of course this pressure on children to do well in school examinations is good for the school. Principals obsess with looking good in the eyes of their peers, the parents and their province.

I endlessly hear principals claiming things like a 99.3% pass rate in Grade 12. So what? Did the children learn anything? Now that would be something worth boasting about. The teachers have a stake in the results as well.

I remember how an anxious mathematics teacher told me that if she had a failure in teaching this subject, she would be 'demoted' (her words) to teaching mathematical literacy. And imagine as a parent being able to boast that your Sipho or Sanna got straight As in the Senior Certificate examination; the genes do wonders! And there you were, thinking that this whole game was about the children or about learning. It is, let me be honest, simply a game.

Nothing demonstrates the demise of learning in our society more powerfully than what happens to poor children in serially disrupted schools and classrooms.

Somewhere around June of the school year, mindless bureaucrats and politicians decide you can cram into weekend and vacation ovens thousands of little facts that children will remember long enough to give back on the date of the dreaded examination.

You do not need to be an educational psychologist to recognise this is not learning; it is the education equivalent of force-feeding an undernourished patient on junk food.

My blood pressure rises dangerously when at the end of a semester of teaching a student raises her hand and asks that uniquely South African question: 'What is the scope of the examination?'

My answer tends to be sarcastic: 'Scope? In my days that was a name for a dirty magazine.'

They don't get it, of course, because every other lecturer plays this game called 'scope'.

I make it clear to these spoilt brats that learning is not possible by selecting things to study because you try to anticipate – aided and abetted by the lecturers – what will be in the examination.

What is the point of learning complex subject matter? It is to understand the subject deeply, to probe, to enquire, and to unsettle. It requires meditation on what you learn and re-examining your most cherished beliefs. At its best, learning is transformation.

The worst measure of such achievement is a standardised test or pressure-cooker examination.

Harsh realities of teaching

What does a violent society teach children about conflict resolution?

4 August 2011

The young boy being kicked and beaten by his principal at the Alberton high school will be assaulted many more times on South African television before the media and its salivating public have had their fill of this dramatic recorded attack.

The airing of the clip over and over again does not add new information, but it feeds our most base emotions of anger, disgust, and even the impulse for retaliation.

What the principal did was wrong, and you do not need the South African Schools Act to tell you that assaulting a child is a serious offence.

Before we climb on our high horses of self-righteousness, let us consider some uncomfortable facts.

There are thousands of teachers across this country who beat the children entrusted to their care every single day, and many more parents tell me brazenly at school or community workshops how they beat their children – using the most bizarre biblical references to back up their cruelty.

This is not the problem of one errant principal – this is the problem of a violent society that now teaches yet another generation of future adults that the way to resolve your problems is by beating those who inconvenience you.

A fired columnist wonders what he did wrong when he attacks one of the most senior editors in the country by saying that, in another time, she would have had a tyre placed around her neck for her criticism of a politician.

Day after day our most senior political leaders rant about opponents using the most vicious language conceivable. Our students take the cue, and across university campuses in the past few months we have witnessed violent behaviour. Before we dump on one principal, take a good look in the mirror.

Why would the principal of this school resort to such harsh and desperate measures? I think I have an idea.

Have you ever been in a school where children threaten teachers with the instruments of violence? Have you ever tried to teach when you can see the drug-crazed eyes of a tortured boy? Have you ever seen the anxiety of a woman teacher with one eye on the open door as she fears what might happen if she dares to challenge a juvenile gangster in her classroom?

Have you ever taught in places where you can literally hear the gunshots around and sometimes on the school grounds? Do you know how difficult it is in South Africa for a school principal or the governing body of a school to expel a disruptive student, even when that child is a routine offender who wrecks the lives of other children and the calmness required for classroom learning?

Now imagine you are the principal of a school in a former white, working-class area on the southern outskirts of Johannesburg.

The white children had long left as black children dominated enrolments. The black youths coming to this school were those who routinely failed inside the township schools of Soweto and surrounds, or were pushed out because of their violent and disruptive behaviour.

They discover another chance inside a distant white school where the discipline quickly crumbles; the white principal leaves, having been threatened for requiring discipline from children who learnt quickly to use the race card to defend their reckless behaviour. Slowly but surely, both black and white pupils with high ambitions for a better life also leave, even if they can't afford it, and the school drowns in a sea of academic mediocrity and the constant threat of violence.

Desperate and at his wits' end, the principal falls back on the only medicine he knows – corporal punishment. And while beating other people's children is no lasting solution, it at least buys temporary relief for stressed teachers. In the pressure cooker of teaching, the beating offers some twisted relief and, importantly, gives the principal the (false) impression that he is still in control of his school.

Nobody has taught this principal the many other ways in which young people from traumatic environments can be disciplined. Few district officials have the knowledge to assist the principal to reorganise the school and its managerial routines so that the critical mix of compassion and constraint is wisely administered.

I feel for the principal.

Politicians must stay out of it

Social cohesion happens on the ground

12 July 2012

On any given school holiday, in the middle of Masi-phumelele, you are likely to find a group of older white youths helping talented black pupils to prepare them for matric examinations and the beginning of university.

Lying between the middle-class suburbs of Fish Hoek and the colourless flats of Ocean View, 'Masi', as some visitors call it, is a tough neighbourhood. Yet the library in the heart of the township is a hive of learning – of everything from mathematics to drama – for some of the smartest kids I've met.

The bond between these deeply committed white youths and their younger black counterparts is something to behold.

This is one of the many places where I discover the practice of social cohesion daily in our talkative country.

We should be very nervous when politicians call conferences on social cohesion. Such platforms are little other than opportunities for political grandstanding.

We should be even more perturbed when those politicians start to dish out history lessons. And so it was. One told us our problems started in 1913, neatly absolving us of what we have not done since 1994.

Another ventured the rather novel insight that the problems of the Western Cape derived from the past. And not a few pointed the familiar finger of accusation at 'the racial other' as we witnessed South Africa's favourite non-racial pastime, self-declared victimhood.

More than one rehashed the tired analogy of sitting on time bombs. Talk, talk, talk.

There is a lot of social cohesion happening in integrated schools, in the new mega churches, in schoolboy rugby, in everyday work relations where ordinary people work hard to find one another, away from the media spotlight on the political gyrations of the powerful.

It happened in the rural Free State, where a black physiotherapy student, as part of his practical work, overcame the racial fear of a *tannie* in a home for the elderly and gave her the best therapeutic massage of her life (her words).

It happened with a farmer who gave away some of his land and cattle, and provided training to emerging black farmers to ensure they maintained productive farms for themselves and their families.

It happened when a black man jumped out of his car to help a blind white woman cross the road as he saw her repeatedly knocking her white stick against the pavement.

It happened when a white woman accepted the threat of estrangement and disinheritance from her conservative family and went right ahead and married her black lover.

These are not fictitious examples. These are events I've witnessed among ordinary South Africans.

It would help enormously if, between talk shops on social cohesion, politicians did not sing threatening and demeaning songs from the past to provoke white people.

It would be helpful if black politicians showed up at the regular funerals of whites murdered on their farms and in their homes.

It would advance the cause of social cohesion if white corporate leaders launched a public manifesto of their commitment to social justice in the workplace.

And it would make a huge difference if the right-wing parties did not try to recreate apartheid by labelling themselves as 'white minorities' on the verge of extinction by a black majority.

In other words, it would advance social cohesion if the politicians stayed out of the way. There will not be another Nelson Mandela who wields the powerful symbols of state and the example of a statesman to demonstrate how we can be and work together for the cause of social justice.

What amazes me about the youth of Masiphumelele is how these new recruits lived through the first semester of university.

All of them boast a bag of distinctions in difficult subjects. They are without the racial bitterness so easily observed in angry students. They are optimistic about their futures and live, learn and love so easily among those with lighter skins.

In that library in 'Masi' they learned not only to do well in their academics but to relate well to their white brothers and sisters who loved them and taught them despite the failings of the schools in the area.

The other day I popped in at the Masi library. I found my current students working alongside their white mentors from previous years.

'Please come and meet my mother,' said one of them. 'She would be so proud.'

Let's read for our kids' sake

Build educational foundations early

6 July 2011

The year is 2044. The government of the day establishes a commission of pro-regime so-called 'experts' who for some reason believe that they can literally plan the country out of trouble.

The planning commission eventually releases a 'diagnostic' report that makes the astounding discovery that 'the quality of education for poor black South Africans is substandard'.

The nation expresses shock at this remarkable finding; the media 'talking heads' heap praise on the minister of planning for her remarkable insight.

A few weeks later, the minister of education releases even more shocking results: our learners from Grades 1 through 6 cannot read or do maths; in fact, the national averages in these two areas of learning fall well below 50%.

The minister makes the prophetic statement that she 'saw this coming', and adds that, while all the international tests over the past decades showed the same levels of underperformance in the country, 'this time we have our very own assessment data'.

The media praises the minister's courage in undertaking these homemade tests, free of foreign interference. The nation is breathless about the promise that 50 years after apartheid we now have the data to really, really, really improve our schools.

I am not sure with whom my sense of dismay is greater – the politicians who make-believe we need more data on the dysfunctional school system in order to improve it, or the uncritical citizens who swallow yet another load of official deception that would have us believe that somehow measuring learners (again and again and again) will miraculously lead to better results the next time round in literacy and numeracy.

We know what is wrong in the foundation years of schooling. Too much time is wasted. Too many teachers are absent. Too few principals lead. Too few parents take an active interest in what happens to reading and calculating after school. Too many policies confuse educators. Too much disruption is caused by unions. Too little accountability is demanded by the government that teachers teach and that schools perform. Too many instructors lack the advanced skills for competent teaching in maths and in literature.

The tragedy of these results is not primarily a function of curriculum; we have fiddled and fumbled with the curriculum for 17 years, and the nett result is the same – the children still cannot read and write.

The last thing we need is yet another curriculum 'statement' that promises to be better than the previous one; the 'new and improved' toothpaste adverts sound more convincing. Ministers have come and gone, each measuring our dilemmas and promising it will be better next time. We remain stuck in the same mess.

It is not only the fact that there is a spectacular lack of imagination in officialdom on how to resolve the problem of low learning achievements in the early years of schooling; it is also the fact that we have come to believe that government can save us. It is time for all of us to do something for the sake of our children.

You could organise a reading hour for primary school children at the nearest library every Saturday morning, say from 9 am to 10 am. If there is no library, use a school or a community centre. Have children read to adults. Have adults read to children. Take turns. Appeal to partners in the private sector to donate books. Bring in entertaining readers like Gcina Mhlophe or others in the community. Award prizes to the best reader, or to the child who reads the most.

Let's do it for the sake of all our children.

How to add for success

The more school, the less maths?

6 December 2012

No, do NOT take your child out of school, yet.

You could be forgiven for reaching the reasonable conclusion that the longer your child stays in school, the less maths she will know. After all, data from the 2012 Annual National Assessments (ANA) for Mathematics for average percentage marks in successive grades reads as follows: Grade 1 (68%), Grade 2 (57%), Grade 3 (41%), Grade 4 (37%), Grade 5 (30%), Grade 6 (27%), Grade 9 (13%).

The minister's response to this disaster?

'To my director general and his team, thank you for a job well done. I am confident the team will again rise to the occasion as you've done in respect of ANA 2012.'

My problem is not with the minister or the entire class of politicians engaged in this game of mass delusion of the people. My problem is with us, ordinary citizens, and our capacity to swallow nonsense of this kind 18 years into a democracy that promised a better education for all our children.

We demand accountability of teachers, but not from those who control R207 billion of expenditure allocated to improve education. We will keep the same people in power no matter how poorly they perform in their portfolios. That says something about us, not about the powerful.

At least this time the ministerial speech did not blame apartheid; there was a more convenient monster at hand: 'The system is now safely sailing out of its [Outcomes-Based Education] OBE troubled waters and moving towards safe waters.'

If you are impressed by clumsy political poetry, enjoy. Those Grade 9s who were part of the 13% national average for the grade in 2012, I suspect will have choice words for this kind of potty verbiage. So what can be done to improve mathematical achievement?

- Stop testing children. To be frank, we did not need yet another test of achievement, or rather under-achievement, to tell us there is a serious crisis in mathematics education. The testing should stop or, if absolutely necessary, should be done every five years, since the money, energy and time swallowed in these annual exercises are already draining the little capacity teachers still have left in a busy school year. Rather direct the resources and energies available into changing maths teaching and learning.

- Test teachers (not learners) in every grade to determine their base levels of mathematical competence for the grade in which they teach; unless we bite this political bullet because government is fearful of powerful unions, I promise you the problem will not go away.

- Use the test data to design mass-based training for all primary school teachers in the basics of mathematics.

- Close schools for a month at the beginning of every year and immerse all teachers in intensive training in the content and pedagogy of mathematics teaching.

- Supervise and mentor the weakest teachers through direct observation and feedback in every classroom to ensure they can teach competently following the intensive training provided; a competent maths mentor in every one of the weakest schools who does nothing else would be the most important investment strategy to turn around performance.
- Remove teachers who, despite intensive training and mentoring, still cannot teach basic maths well and place them elsewhere in the education department's vast bureaucracy, but not in a classroom.
- Issue a certificate or licence of competency to teach mathematics to every teacher who, after training, supervision and mentoring, can teach at the levels required; no teacher should be allowed to teach the subject without such a real certificate of competence.
- Generate basic learning materials that allow for repetitive practice (drill, in other words, and to hell with the constructivists and other fancy theorists who believe the answers must be 'discovered') in the solution of basic mathematical problems in every grade.
- Give maths homework every day and give feedback on that homework every morning. Homework is still one of the best strategies for improving scholastic achievement, especially in poor schools.
- Mobilise parents around every school to become part of the homework as supervisors of time spent on homework every day in maths; in the process, many parents might also learn to do basic mathematics, as in

the Family Math & Family Science projects operating at one university.

These are simple, time-honoured strategies backed by the best research that offer game-breaking strategies to end this stalemate in education. Whether there is the political will to drive such a strategy from the centre is the main question.

We can do the maths

Maths literacy is an insult to education

8 November 2012

If you still believe mathematical literacy should remain in the school curriculum, consider the following question from the Grade 12 Mathematical Literacy Paper 1 examination written last week: 'State whether the following event is CERTAIN, MOST LIKELY or IMPOSSIBLE: Christmas Day is on December 25 in South Africa.'

For this brainteaser you would gain two marks. I am not sure what upsets me more – the fact that there are three options to this question, the cultural bias against non-Christian pupils, or that the mathematics in question 1.1.7 is not obvious at all.

Then, if that were not enough, Statistics South Africa released its *Census 2011* report which, on its front cover, shows a smiling young teacher with chalk and duster in hand addressing a group of schoolchildren. Behind her is a blackboard showing division problems, one below the other. Question 3 shows a line that reads 21 ÷ 7 = 6. Whether this is poor use of the blackboard space or a simple error of calculation, the carelessness of mathematical representation speaks to the broader crisis of maths and science in our country. That Stats SA did not realise the embarrassing front-page message makes you wonder about the reliability of what appears between the covers.

Small wonder the fifth *Financial Development Report of the World Economic Forum*, also released last week, placed South Africa last out of 62 countries for the quality of its science and mathematics education. Ahead of us were poor countries like Kenya, Bangladesh, Ghana and Nigeria. A good friend told of a countryman who saw the forum's announcement in a positive light – we got 100%: 62 out of 62.

Fret not; there is wonderful news just released. The minister of basic education will appoint a committee to investigate the standard of the matric exams. Don't hold your breath; I can confidently give you the results of that investigation in advance. The study will not declare the matric standards a disaster; they will report that our standards are actually quite high and on a par with other countries, but perhaps minor adjustments need to be made. It is called politics; when under pressure, establish a commission.

In the meantime, the foundations of mathematics teaching and learning remain a crisis and no amount of testing and retesting will change that fact.

Here are three simple realities: Most primary school teachers do not know enough maths to teach it (content), they do not know enough about the teaching of maths to teach the subject effectively (pedagogy) and they do not work in stable school contexts to teach without interruption (instructional time).

This brings me to the story of Thembi* (a pseudonym), which I share with you in 'Girl's Journey from Horror to Triumph' (see page 271). I was deeply moved, and at times emotional, as scores of South Africans at home and abroad sent emails offering to contribute to the university education of this remarkable young matriculant who not only survived the horror of rape and bearing witness to the murder of her mother at the hands of her father, but rose above these traumas to score her highest marks this year (90%, 94%) in not one but two mathematics papers.

Many readers said they were pensioners, and one asked: 'Would you mind if I gave R20 only? It's all I have.' A mother shared the story with her child, who also wanted to contribute from his meagre pocket money. Others said they had no money at all as they were unemployed. 'But I will pray for her,' said one, and from another jobless person: 'Can I read to her or help in any other way?'

The commitments still come daily, and I want to thank you sincerely on behalf of the young woman; she will write to you after the Grade 12 exams are over.

I can assure you there are millions of young women like Thembi out there who, given half a chance at a decent maths education, will also excel in this subject with quality teaching in stable school environments. What grieves me deeply is the amount of talent that is wasted because our expectations of youths are so low.

Yet your responses prove to me what is possible with citizen action. Just imagine that the energy, commitment and selflessness that you demonstrated were used to change all our schools and improve the academic prospects of every student across the country.

What if, as you showed, our first response to an education crisis somewhere was not our incorrigibly fractious government but our own resources – spiritual, emotional, intellectual and material?

For now, be certain to enjoy December 25.

Here's the blunt truth

We need real educational solutions, not more policies

25 October 2012

One of the most serious errors committed by overzealous politicians in South Africa is to use education policy as a blunt instrument to solve complex problems that require fine-tuned strategies for change.

This is why the education sector has produced more policies than any other with the least to show for all this activism in terms of learning outcomes. The most recent 'blunt instrument' being proposed is for South Africa to move its three-year degrees to four-year qualifications.

One of the most common reasons given for extending the degree by a year is the fact that the school system produces weak academic students who require an additional year of study. In other words, the additional year has a compensatory function. The instrument is blunt because not all schools produce weak students, and not all high school graduates require, by this levelling logic, an extra year. But in the mind of zealous ideologues, unless you can impose misery on all students (in this case), it cannot be fair.

Most parents and students already find it very difficult to pay for three years of study. It breaks the heart to see students dropping out of the system after all desperate measures to find money have failed. Many students leave in the final year with good academic marks, unable to raise the last funds required to complete the third year. For such students, adding a fourth year would be an unbearable financial hardship. Of course, a blunt instrument makes no such distinction.

The third reason we should be cautious about adding another year to the degree is one of content. In other words, what exactly should the substance be of that extended curriculum? Should it be catch-up work in basic maths and science or reading and writing? If so, a standard academic degree should not be compromised to make up for endemic failures in the school system.

The message to government should be clear: instead of extending school failure into universities, fix the schools. To use an example from my other pet peeve on our public roads: instead of erecting expensive signs warning about potholes, use the money to fix the damn potholes.

Here is an important warning: the more our universities become expensive compensatory colleges for what the schools do wrong, the less competitive they will become in their global positioning as serious post-school institutions. Already universities divert significant resources and energy into serving – as we should – larger segments of talented students with poor school preparation. To now institutionalise this failure of schools in a four-year degree would be to spread the mediocrity into formal qualifications.

Most universities already have an additional year or two of academic preparation only for those students who lack the basic competencies to enter a formal science or humanities degree straight out of high school. This system works well in universities that take seriously curriculum commitments such as small-group instruction, disciplinary competence and basic academic skills. These pre-degree years build competence and confidence among students and ensure that those who eventually take the degree also succeed. We have solid data to show this model works especially for first-generation university students.

I would support a four-year degree on grounds of academic advancement rather than historical compensation. For example, a strong 'liberal arts' degree that educates students broadly by engaging the big intellectual questions of the day would constitute a powerful additional year in a university system in which students specialise too early. At the present time they are trained long before they are educated. I have never understood why a first-year student straight out of high school must immediately do courses in engineering or anthropology or biochemistry.

When we recently sent some of our top undergraduate students to sit in classes at leading universities in the world, I asked them what the one difference is between students from that country and South African students. Their answers were consistent: they know much more about everything than we do. That is a case for a four-year degree.

Students will resist such a broader education for a simple reason – since high school they have been taught to think narrowly in preparation for examinations. The laughable boot camps of the past few months, in which students are force-fed exam questions and answers to make up for lost time during the year, is an example of how we devalue the education of our children. The Annual National Assessments take this obsession with testing narrow knowledge down to the lower grades of primary school.

A four-year degree must require that we fundamentally rethink the education of our smartest youths in the context of a 21st-century global economy in which our best minds can compete.

Time to raise the bar

Campaign for a 50% pass rate in all subjects

17 May 2012

Presently pupils in high school are allowed to pass three of the Grade 12 subjects at 30% and two with 40% and still qualify to obtain a National Senior Certificate and, with the right combination of passes, gain entry into university. This is dangerous and debilitating for the following reasons.

One, the signal sent by these very low standards for achievement is that we have low expectations of ourselves and of what we as a society can achieve.

We tell young people that, in theory, they can be ignorant of 70% (or 60%) of the subject matter content and that this is acceptable.

We tell employers not to expect too much of high school graduates, and we signal to universities that these destructively low standards should not bar entry to higher learning. In short, we demean ourselves and, to be frank, we play right into the hands of what was in fact the intention of our apartheid masters: to keep black people in constant subjugation.

Two, these low standards will position South Africa as losers in a globally competitive economy.

At a time when emerging economies are strengthening their education systems in a fast-changing world, South

Africa is going in the opposite direction. We aspire to be a leader in Africa, and we complain bitterly when the West speaks for the developing world.

But the way to speak with authority among leading nations is from a position of strength, not weakness. Stagnating at 30/40 (pass percentage) runs the risk of condemning Africa's strongest economy and still most-promising democracy to an afterthought in history.

Three, the 30/40 arrangement will maintain two classes (in both senses of the word) of school performers. This arrangement benefits mainly the black poor, to phrase the dilemma bluntly.

The deracialised middle classes in the better one-third of schools – by resources and functionality – will continue to amass high pass rates and subject distinctions while we give false security to the masses in dysfunctional schools that they too have passed; in fact, they have failed.

Education remains the best instrument for closing the socioeconomic inequalities that separate these two classes of schools in the country.

I am certainly not suggesting that the education authorities artificially inflate the 30/40 arrangement to 50%; quite the opposite.

The 50% standard of achievement should be used to ensure government meets the input standards (qualified teachers, textbooks for every child, basic infrastructure and so on) and process standards (predictable school timetables, teachers on task for every lesson, every day and so on) to ensure that this barely respectable minimum of education achievement becomes a reality for all our children.

In other words, the 50% position is a measure of accountability for the state to deliver on its provisioning mandate rather than to celebrate the systematic 'dumbing down' of the youth on the basis of low standards.

In this regard the campaign by Equal Education to hold provincial governments accountable for minimum standards of provisioning fits right into the logic of the 50% campaign. The standards set are not only for pupils but for all of us in the education chain of command: government, principals, teachers, and then only the pupils.

I understand the migration towards 50% will need to be gradual for the simple reason that it will be a major political embarrassment for the government and the ruling party when tens of thousands of additional pupils fail.

I propose we start with abandoning the 30% passing level immediately (applied in 2013), and then gradually push the standard passing levels up by 5% every year so that by 2015 we would have established the new norm of 50% for passing in all school subjects.

There is an important psychological motivation for this position that we can bank on.

When nations set their standards high, systems respond to the higher demands. Young people who receive the consistent message that we expect more from them, that we trust them to do better, tend to rise to those adult expectations.

Teachers and principals will adjust to the new demands, knowing their reputations as professionals require aiming higher rather than pushing unsuspecting pupils over the lower bars.

Universities and employers will begin to trust the products of our education system, and fewer independent schools will jettison the state examinations.

At the heart of the 50% campaign is my deep belief that we can do better as a nation, and that we have not even begun to take advantage of the tremendous capability of all our young people.

Where are all the natives?

Why are fewer and fewer South Africans getting high-level university degrees?

26 April 2012

We are running out of educated natives.

No other demographic trend in education is more damning than this: not only are fewer South Africans coming through the school and university system, but they are also slowly being replaced by African immigrants.

Perhaps nobody noticed the consistent decline in the number of pupils entering the Grade 12 examinations: from more than 600 000 in 2008 to just over 500 000 in 2011.

Taken together over a four-year period, 2 251 555 students entered the matriculation year between 2008 and 2011, but only 1 381 020 eventually passed, a loss of 80 535 youths who either failed or did not write. In the next year or two, that loss will rise to 1 million young people lost since 2008.

The evidence of this collapse in numbers is to be found at the point of production of high-level skills at the end of the university cycle, that is, the doctorate.

Almost half the African women PhDs graduating from our universities are not South African.

In fact, the percentage share of foreign doctoral graduates in South Africa (27%), says a recent report, is higher than the share of such graduating students in Japan (16.8%), Sweden (20.6%) and the US (26.3%).

For a developing country, this is bad news. Of course, the rot starts in the school system: the fewer students who graduate from school, the fewer enrol in university, and even fewer still continue into honours, masters and doctoral degrees. The pipeline contains a slowing trickle of talent with dire consequences for a country that wishes to boost economic development by strengthening the base of human capital at the upper end of the training ladder.

The growth in foreign talent in our universities is of course a good thing, given that we have been isolated for too long from academic networks in other parts of the continent and the world.

Global universities thrive on borderless talent, not on some language or ethnic nationalism that consumes, and indeed destroys, institutions of higher learning.

But there is a serious downside to these numbers in a country obsessed before and since 1994 with racial nationalism. The growing number of non-nationals with PhDs comes from poor African countries and many would prefer to live and work in South Africa.

These are highly talented academics, professionals and business people who would slowly, but surely, occupy leading positions in the post-apartheid workplace. The problem, as indicated, lies in the feeder system, and this weak stream of students into postgraduate studies is particularly acute in the case of black graduates.

This trend is going to drive the government insane because it will not satisfy the native grunt for 'Africans in particular' in the boardrooms of companies and senates of universities.

Recriminations will flow fast and furiously; whites will be to blame and coloureds will again be declared to be in oversupply.

Instead of putting their finger on the root of the problem – a dysfunctional school system for the majority – there will be pressure for solutions here and now and, in their failure to satisfy ethnic urges, expect a healthy outbreak of academic and corporate xenophobia. In other words, the resentment will shift from targeting Somalis and Pakistanis in township shops to targeting the African middle classes in the cities who come from elsewhere.

In the long term, we need, of course, to rebuild the school system so that more native students enter, write and pass the terminal examinations at higher levels of performance. There are no shortcuts to building a high-quality school system that feeds graduates into a high-quality university system that produces more postgraduate students.

These trends require a radically different strategy for securing South Africa's competitiveness in a global economy where knowledge matters more than ever before.

We should, in my view, follow the example of the next great global university, the Okinawa Institute of Science and Technology in Japan. The government subsidy of this world-class institution is dependent on meeting this critical requirement: fewer than half the professors must be from Japan.

When you walk into its labs, you are more likely to meet scholars from non-Japanese universities in countries such as Poland, Britain, Canada, Australia, China, Korea and the US.

When you enter the grounds of this prestigious campus you will be greeted by a world-class particle physicist who introduces himself as president of the university.

He is from Cape Town.

Seven costly mistakes

Is education in South Africa worse now than under apartheid?

5 April 2012

Mamphela Ramphele has nothing to lose. As a semi-retired older woman with a more-than-sufficient pension fund, she is not dependent on anyone, let alone the ruling party, for a job.

As a former activist with impeccable struggle credentials, she commands attention. So when the former World Bank vice-president says education was better under apartheid than it is today, more than a few angry politicians would be singing '*Umshini wami*'.

Is she right?

It is almost two decades since the start of a major shake-up in education in South Africa, and to understand the state of schools, colleges and universities today, we need to understand how we got here.

Of course, the long shadow of apartheid continues to haunt present-day education, especially with respect to the gross inequality that separates the top 20% of well-functioning, well-resourced public schools from the mess that constitutes the remaining 80% of schools.

But it would be disingenuous to blame this mess only on the apartheid legacy. We have had almost 20 years to begin fixing the problem.

What did we do, and fail to do, that made Ramphele issue this astounding claim? Specifically, what were the seven major mistakes made in education since the mid-1990s?

Mistake number one must be Outcomes-Based Education. Even government agrees it was a mistake, and who can forget the current minister of basic education trying desperately to deny support for these sweeping curricular changes? But think of the financial and operational costs. Almost 30 000 schools were misled into thinking that, by adopting this complex curriculum plan, teaching and learning would improve. Instead, scholastic achievement is worse than ever, from literacy and numeracy in the foundation years to the disastrous National Senior Certificate results in Grade 12.

Mistake number two must be the indiscriminate voluntary severance packages offered to teachers at the dawn of democracy. To be fair, this hare-brained scheme started even before 1994, but the new government implemented it in an attempt to 'rightsize' the teaching corps and save money. The result? The best teachers left the system. The teachers who remained behind, especially in the most disadvantaged schools, were in general those with weaker teaching qualifications and less experience than those who left.

Mistake number three was closing good teacher education colleges. Let me be clear; some of the colleges had to be closed. Colleges in the homelands produced the worst teachers. But there were good colleges, like the Johannesburg College of Education, the Normaal Kollege Pretoria, the Giyani Teachers College and the Bellville Teachers College. But for a government with a reform hammer that sees all problems as nails, all the colleges were shut down or incorporated into universities. That was a mistake, for universities are not the best places for training primary school teachers.

Mistake number four was the irrational mergers of some universities that made absolutely no sense. The merger of Medunsa, a medical school in Pretoria, with the University of the North in Polokwane, made no sense for reasons of geographical, political and emotional distance. It should have been merged with the medical school at Tukkies, down the road, as was the case with the veterinary sciences.

Mistake number five was the merger of universities with technikons to constitute what government calls comprehensive universities. Ask ten senior people in higher education what a comprehensive university is, and you will get ten different answers. We decided on mergers for political reasons, and then, after the act, queried what we should call them. Technikons should have stayed as top-quality technical institutions offering world-class technical qualifications, not quasi-universities pretending to pursue university-type research.

Mistake number six was neglect of mother-tongue instruction, especially in township schools. A solid foundation is required in the mother tongue to ease the later transition to the national universities. The black middle classes sent their children to non-mother-tongue schools, in part to escape the tragedy of dysfunctional schools. In the process, our children lacked solid grounding in any language, a prerequisite for strong academic learning.

Mistake number seven was the failure to install basic minimum standards for school education which were legally enforceable. The legal notion of 'adequacy' in the funding of schools that applies in countries like the US does not apply here. As a consequence, nobody can be held accountable for the huge discrepancies in infrastructure among different schools.

Through a combination of legacy, neglect and bad policy decisions, our educational institutions are indeed in a worse state than before.

The future looks bleak

Predictions for the future of our education system

15 March 2012

It is the question I am asked most often across the length and breadth of the country: If you had a crystal ball, what does the future of education look like in South Africa?

You do not need magical powers to see the near or long-term future of the country, so here are my predictions about what to expect of education going forward.

- The political calculus favours the status quo. It is clear that in the current arrangements in which the most disadvantaged schools are held hostage by powerful unions (such as in the Eastern Cape), and where teaching and learning can be switched on or off by an educators' strike, it is not desirable for government to intervene.

The union is tied to the powerful alliance which has, over the years, become a major factor in determining the futures of senior politicians. No cabinet minister, or even the president, is going to take on this power bloc frontally.

For this reason, the balance of forces, to coin a phrase, ensures the poorest schools remain the playground for union control into the foreseeable future. In this scenario, learners take a back seat to the material interests of organised teachers.

- The socioeconomic arrangements in the country favour greater inequality over time. This is very bad news, with a twist. The growing inequality will be based on class rather than race as a small but growing elite of black parents send their children into deracialised, former white middle-class schools, leaving behind the masses of poor black children in the large, disadvantaged education pool.

Race then resolves itself as a problem in middle-class schools, and over time many (not all) of these former white schools will become majority black, but will retain the achievement cultures of these schools.

What does not change are the fortunes of the poor, colour apart. This is what wise people refer to when they talk about the ticking time bomb facing our country.

- The poor, marginalised schools become sites of growing unrest and rebellion as young people sense that they have been sold out by their government.

These poor students would bear witness, daily, to schools that work and other youths that excel, and it would dawn on them that their chances of escaping poverty cannot be explained away by apartheid alone, but by calculated neglect by the people they put into power, and whose own children sit in that small tier of settled middle-class schools.

- The stagnation among poor youths in schools becomes a happy hunting ground for politically organised youths who fuel rebellion, which is carried over into universities for those who scrape through school given the questionable standards of school-leaving certificates.

Those universities that enrol the majority of these students from neglected schools become the prime targets of chronic rebellion which increasingly blurs the distinction between a morally defensible protest and outright thuggery.

Higher education becomes solidified into two subsystems: a racially integrated university subsystem among the research-intensive institutions, and a larger, black subsystem trapped in cycles of student upheaval alongside financial and managerial crises.

- The education system will experience an increasing irrelevance of a host of reforms that, while they serve symbolic ends and convey the pretence of being serious about change, in fact fail to disrupt 'the grammar of schooling' – that hard core of education functions or dysfunctions that define a school as good or bad.

There is a sense of this irrelevance in recent pronouncements of new universities, dragging kids to the police for coming late, imposing an African language in the university curriculum, and requiring a central applications system for university enrolments. None of the proposals are, in and of themselves, undesirable.

The point is that none of these supposed interventions deal with the real problems of inequality and systemic dysfunction in the school or university systems.

- The education of young people will increasingly be held together, especially in poorer schools, by the moral underground of initiatives by non-governmental organisations, churches, corporate entities and even some universities.

From literacy and numeracy initiatives to science and maths projects to special access programmes to higher education – all funded from external sources – a barely functional educational system will be prevented from complete implosion. But since none of these initiatives are large and central enough to drive systemic change, the overall system will remain in a state of stable crisis well into the future.

Not a pretty picture.

Teaching academics the art

Most university professors can't teach, but don't know it

7 December 2011

They attained their PhDs in fields such as chemistry or economics or labour law to prove that they could do research and advance knowledge in their fields.

Except for the few who studied and practised teaching, academics in general have no clue how to teach. Except they do not know that.

Because everyone can open their mouths and utter words, academics think they can teach. Because our society has so demeaned the complex science and art of teaching, any idiot with a book in his or her hand believes that he or she can convey the profound truths of a discipline.

What passes for teaching in many of our universities would scare the paying public. I have seen academics download Wikipedia scraps as official class materials. I have seen thoughtless lecturers repeat the same examination questions year after year.

I still see antediluvian creatures using overhead projectors in classes packed with 'millennials' who prefer using iPads as their preferred mode of engaging the worlds around them. I have grown tired of seeing witless scholars reading from textbooks – a task students could have done in bed after downloading an ebook.

When a student can pass a course based simply on the notes handed out by a teacher, they have been short-changed in teaching.

The purpose of teaching is to open up the mind; to challenge preconceptions; to destabilise everyday truths; to sharpen the capacity to question; to broaden the scope of what is known; to instil the habits of thought and to open up the sheer joy of learning.

The culture of 'notes' and 'note-taking' has a very different purpose – to prepare you to write and pass an exam without stretching the mind beyond what is expected.

'I have a different view to my lecturer on this topic,' my student daughter told me recently.

'But the lecturer made it clear that she only wants back what she gave us in class.'

I hear this all the time from students across the country.

There is, of course, a good reason for this 'dumbing down' of university teaching. University managers place huge pressure on academics to reverse what they call 'low throughput rates' for one simple reason – the more students fail, the less the institutions can collect in state subsidy returns. Of course I understand such an impulse.

But does that mean we sell our intellectual souls to the subsidy devil? Does that mean we reduce the teaching of university graduates to the production of a quota of canned foods from a factory plant?

The demise of university teaching has serious implications for democracy for one simple reason: the university might be the only remaining space in which young people could be confronted with their prejudices, where received knowledge can be disrupted, and where a new value system for future leaders could be ingrained.

When a university hands out a degree without any guarantee of the value added to the recipient's education, you sustain the uncritical, herd mentality of obedient parliamentarians where a conscience vote or an independent view on the 'Secrecy Bill' would have you insulted as 'a free agent'.

'The value of your degree,' I told students at our recent graduation, 'hinges on two questions: Did we teach you to think for yourself? And did we teach you to give of yourself?'

I reminded them how easy it is to buy a degree off the Internet, and that where you study makes all the difference.

Smart universities now have centres for teaching and learning to teach professors how to teach.

Smart universities shift their resources from the social welfarism that concentrates teaching on playing 'catch-up' with the weakest students from the school system to engaging all university students in higher learning.

Smart universities no longer evaluate professors only for their research performance but also for their teaching abilities. Smart universities no longer pump their students full of knowledge but on a regular basis ask fundamental questions such as: 'What is a university education for?'

Smart universities now insist their professors (and not recent honours graduates) are included among those who teach first-year undergraduate students.

When you choose with your child a university for 2012, be bold and ask the university officers: 'How serious are you about undergraduate teaching?'

Your choices will be sharply limited to a handful of universities and, inside of them, to a handful of programmes.

Jeppe pride lives on

A school to restore your faith in good old-values public schooling

8 March 2012

If you've lost all faith in good old-values public schooling, and were considering moving your children out of this country, do not make that decision until you have visited South Africa's most-fabled high school on the appropriately named Good Hope Street in Johannesburg.

Every student tiptoes around the large emblem and motto of the school engraved in the cement just inside the front door: *Forti nihil difficilius*. You can smell the history of the school in the main hall, with its old wooden floors and black-and-white photographs of men's sporting teams dating back to the early part of the previous century.

I knew I was in a special place.

Unlike all the famous old public schools I have visited, this one has the least pretence. Everything looks ordinary, even cheap. Many of the boys are from struggling families; several from working-class backgrounds. All the stuff in the principal's office could sell for less than R1 000 to a generous buyer.

Even the striped black-and-white blazers look second-hand.

The hall is under construction so I have to speak to the 800-odd boys in the blazing sun outside. Yet the school oozes culture, values and self-belief like I have never seen anywhere else. All boys, big and small, stop to greet the overweight black stranger on their premises.

A respectful and emphatic 'sir' is a common word in every space on this sprawling campus with its impressive sports fields.

This, after all, is Jeppe Boys.

And so I steer the conversation to its most famous teacher, Jake White, the World Cup-winning rugby coach. I am greeted by its most famous unofficial teacher, the elderly Mr Ledwaba, who doubles as a science laboratory assistant, though his real job is caretaker.

Ledwaba, who obtained his science degree last year, points proudly at the plaque reading 'The Ledwaba Stairs' that leads into the main building.

Every old school has a powerful narrative that defines its core identity. For Jeppe, it is the story of the Jackson clan, whose father arrived at the door of the school many years ago, an orphan from Rhodesia who was shunted to Durban and then to Johannesburg, with nothing at all.

The school turned an orphan into a decent man whose sons also attended Jeppe. It is a story of how a poor boy can become a decent man.

It is the story of Jeppe. Its website declares proudly what no other English school has as a line of distinction: 'Jeppe has never been an elitist school'. The Theo Jackson Scholarship Fund supports poor boys; sports and academics are not that important, says the fund. Character is. That story of struggle and the virtue of character run like a golden thread through the history of Johannesburg's oldest high school since the

1890s, when it experienced financial difficulties after the school was closed for the duration of the Anglo-Boer War.

It is that badge of struggle, that nothing comes easily, that character is everything, that is written into the Latin motto (at the start of this piece): 'For the brave nothing is too difficult'.

Jeppe is a reminder of how the story of struggle can become the foundation of enduring values of gratitude, generosity and goodness rather than of justified greed: ('I did not struggle to be poor') and the impulse for selfishness ('It's our time to eat').

Solid as a rock, this school, which has lost old boys to at least three wars, tells the struggle narrative differently, with humility and with a sense of service to others.

In a centenary year for an important political party, Jeppe offers a model of how to tell the story of a difficult past that can enhance the greatness of an institution by retaining at the centre its founding values. Now, confronted with an army of boys on the stands, I remind them of the values of a good public education, of how the spirit of humanity can triumph over the emptiness of materialism, and of how the privilege of being in a good school carries with it a sense of responsibility to the less privileged.

Then, the fearsome war cry.

In this most racially integrated of public schools, the boys lock into each other around the shoulders, and move slowly from side to side as a whisper becomes a deafening crescendo of manly sounds. The opening line catches my attention: 'All we see is the black and white'.

I think I know what they mean.

Brains must beat fists

An end to violence on our university campuses

1 March 2012

This week an education (believe it or not) student on the Mthatha campus of an Eastern Cape university stepped through a plastic skylight and fell to his death while his mates burnt tyres in the streets, stoned police and vandalised buildings.

Their demands?

They insist on being passed even though they have failed exams.

Prior to that, a spasm of violence spread across a Durban campus as riot police struggled to contain a crowd of belligerent youths whose student leader would spend a night in the dangerous Westville Prison.

Who can forget the image of a cowering female student blanketed in the white froth of a fire extinguisher behind a male student threatening violence with the covered face of a coward?

A Cape Town university student collapses and is rushed to hospital after inhaling pepper spray used to disperse students who attacked security guards; at a Potchefstroom university campus, a student was left behind, found dead at the bottom of a university swimming pool after an alleged initiation ritual.

A Johannesburg student saw his mother crushed to death by other students while trying to register for his first year of study last month.

All of this within the first two months of the 2012 academic year in South Africa. The mounting body count is too high. This dreadful cycle of violence has to stop.

Why does this violence among university youths continue, and why does it so often become deadly?

The first reason is the lack of an authoritative voice of leadership that can condemn the violence.

Many of the protesters claim allegiance to political organisations. This means there must be a clear, unequivocal voice of condemnation that spreads throughout the student body on all 23 campuses that violence will not be tolerated.

The deafening silence of the political masters of these students is what gives the youth the message that they can act with impunity.

That clear voice of leadership is often lacking among us as university leaders. When last did you hear a university leader stand up in the public square and condemn student violence out of hand?

Without public leadership that speaks out, expect such wanton violence to continue.

The second reason is the failure of universities to deal effectively with the underlying demands of desperate students. The lack of financial aid lies at the root of the spiralling violence on campus.

When universities have exhausted their own meagre funds, and when the government-funded National Student Financial Aid Scheme runs out of money, students do not target government – they target their universities.

In the long run, the biggest threat to stable campuses in which young people can learn without the threat of constant disruption or study without fear of their physical well-being, is when there is adequacy in the financial aid allocations to deserving students. Strong, proactive management of student funding, clear and consistent communication about the limits of funding, and compassionate policies and plans that ensure that no academically deserving student is disallowed academic access, together reduce the likelihood of violence.

The third reason is the failure of both universities and government to embed in institutional life clear norms for student behaviour.

The sad reality is that most of the students who protest are those who fail repeatedly without policies – or implemented policies – that prevent this from happening.

I have been astounded at how a student can ransack a place of higher learning because he demands readmission after eight years of failure to obtain a three-year degree.

I know for a fact that some of the most destructive student leaders are fully funded by outside political parties because their role is to be either the enforcers or the resisters of 'transformation' on university campuses. It's for this reason that there is such silence on the part of political leaders, of all stripes, when deadly violence ensues. A university is not an island separated from the often violent, convulsive protests in communities outside the campus. Yet a place of higher learning must be countercultural and set a standard for human behaviour that meets two requirements.

One, encouragement of protests, dialogue, and disagreement on the key social problems of the day. This is fundamental to learning the habits of democracy on campuses. Two, the insistence on respect, tolerance and non-destructive behaviour in a place that privileges the head over the fist.

Funding is more vital

Educational priorities for South Africa

16 February 2012

There are different ways of reading the recent State of the Nation address by President Jacob Zuma, one of which is to take word frequency as an imperfect test of official priorities.

The salutations acknowledging dignitaries contain more than 150 words, recognising everyone from visiting officials to former presidents, but the words 'school' and 'university' or 'college' only appear once each. The word 'history' or the phrase 'the past' appears six times, but the word 'future' only once. The word 'quality' is completely absent but the word 'inequality' shows up eight times.

These kinds of public address showpieces are, of course, a political cut-and-paste, and there would have been all kinds of interests and groupings insisting that the president 'say something about' one or other policy or political interest. Still, the combination of words tells us clearly that this is a government still mired in a horrible past, and fighting fires in the present, without a compelling vision of what the future could look like for all of us.

In terms of delivery, the consensus seems to be that the president did much better than in previous performances. But I am curious about content, and especially about our political leader's sense of 'the state of education' in the nation and, of course, what he is going to do about it.

I know the president is not an expert on education, but as a leader he surely must have some basic instincts of what is complex, false or simply unachievable in the lobbied paragraphs on education. Our leader's speech is composed as if the damaging Eastern Cape teachers' strike did not happen, but let me focus on one proposal in a single line for which R300 million has purportedly been set aside.

The two new universities must surely be the most improbable policy position that any government could hold. What on earth is so compelling about a university in every province? Does it matter that the Northern Cape is so sparsely populated that its few high school graduates are an imperceptible number among students in the two closest regional universities?

Does it matter that the attempts at university cooperation with colleges in Mpumalanga fell on hard times because of the unbelievably poor quality of the small numbers of remaining students in the former teacher-education institutions of the former homelands?

The two proposed new universities are not a good idea, and work against the interests of the black poor in those provinces for the following reasons.

One, it takes billions of rand to establish a university with even a modest range of infrastructures, disciplines and expertise – and about R1 billion in the annual budget to sustain a small-to-medium-sized university of quality.

Now one could seriously underspend on such an initiative or simply host two or three academic fields, but then it is hardly a universe of knowledge on offer or a quality post-school site of higher learning.

Two, existing universities already struggle to sustain themselves given massive backlogs in infrastructure – despite a generous spend by the current government after years of neglect. The 23 universities cannot find the quality expertise to teach across disciplines at the levels required. We poach from one another and hire from outside our borders as more and more of a younger generation of academics – especially black talent – find easier vocations in the private sector for a whole lot more money.

So where, exactly, will this high-level expertise come from, without even taking into account the bureaucratic visits from the department of labour to harass institutions on face equity?

Three, the talented students from these two provinces have been easily accommodated in the nearest regional universities for decades. Rather than establish new universities, how about investing additional funding for residential placements from these two provinces at established institutions, and increasing the funding available to all existing students through the national student financing plan?

There are thousands of students, right now, who have excellent academic records but can't find funds from the national plan or whatever source to continue their studies. Institutional budgets are exhausted, and provinces try hard from their meagre funds to finance individual students from their regions. Institutions spend time managing and pre-empting destructive protests from students who argue, rightly, that they kept up their side of the bargain (good academic results) and that government has not released enough money to support them.

Two new universities, underfunded and understaffed, is a recipe for educational failure and an invitation for political instability when students find out they got less than what they bargained for.

WE NEED TO ACT FOR THE FUTURE

'I blame the adults for messing up the futures of our most vulnerable children…'

Slow healing as we transform

Slow changes in unexpected places

1 December 2011

The young man sitting at the lunch table with 15 fellow students had no arms. Next to him sat a woman student who had returned with the group from a short period of studying overseas.

The returnees were excitedly sharing their experiences with us. Every time the young man looked at his friend sitting next to him, she would lift a spoon of food to his mouth. This went on for a while. Just across the road from where this act of communion was playing out, a terrible racial incident nearly destroyed this old university. To-day, the black student is being fed by his friend, the white woman student, as if this was the most natural thing in the world.

'How come there was this old, brown car parked in my driveway?' I ask inside the house.

'A man from the garage dropped off the car. Said it was the address where the car should be delivered after it was serviced.'

I look inside the car, find an address, and drive my own car to what I hope is the natural home of the brown car. It is now dark. I press the buzzer outside the gate. The young man striding down the long path towards my car looks upset once he colours me in.

'What do you want here? Can't you see it's late? Yes?'

I know in his Afrikaans culture this kind of dismissive, angry tone would not have been used if I was white; this knowledge helps the response.

Firmly, and in Afrikaans, I put it to him that I do not talk to disrespectful kids: 'Go call your parents, now!'

Both language and tone surprise him, and he steps back. The parents emerge and recognise me as the university principal; they offer nothing but kindness.

'I need your son for 15 minutes.'

He climbs into the car and we drive to my home where I offer him coffee before giving him the key to drive their car home. He spends all the time apologising for his behaviour.

Inside the beautiful School of Music at the university, a good, old European man has found what he calls raw talent from the townships, training young black teenagers to sing the most beautiful Italian classics.

'It is the songs they choose,' he tries to persuade me, and the youngsters are clearly talented.

In a moment of hush, he exclaims: 'They sing from the natural environment from which they emerge.'

The 'they' rings in the ears as the 'us' absorbs the sweet melodies; the *naturelle* are still with us. This is the ticket for very disadvantaged youths to enter a preliminary university programme in music. The tuition is free; the voice trainers are volunteers; the paternalism, the sense of uplifting mission, of 'them', is there too.

The angry black political leader from outside campus demands more transformation from the university, when what he really wants is ethnic domination. I remind him that every time he meets with the university management it is with an exclusive caste of African men.

'And you want to talk to me about transformation?'

Of course it should not matter in a normal society who he travels with, but normal is still far off, and the hypocrisy of calling for transformation without the capacity for self-reflection is something we need to point out.

Now standing in front of me is one of the most amazing students I have ever met. Only a year ago she was the first black head girl in an overwhelmingly white girls school that still calls itself 'Christian and National' in the public-school system. From inside an aged institution with all the trappings of conservative ideologies from a harmful past, this school, called Orange, after its Dutch colonial roots, recognised, nurtured and brought to leadership a confident, super-intelligent black woman whose first-year university scores average in the 90s. I put my head on a block to say that she will emerge as a major leader in this country in the future.

It is a short flight from the city of roses to that cosmopolitan noisiness called Durban. Today there is a difference. There is no longer the reassuring, deep, white male voice of the pilot introducing the black or woman co-pilot. For the first time, it is a woman introducing her co-pilot, another woman, for the short flight over the Lesotho mountains.

This country changes slowly, in unexpected places, with all the scars of a wounded past, awkwardly and painfully. But away from the noise of succession and secrecy bills, we transform anyway.

School not for sissies

Learn for more than exams at school

10 November 2011

During the early years I was hopeless at everything in school. I was the first boy in the history of my school to be lapped in the 400 m race. 'How,' you ask, 'is that possible when this is a one-lap race?'

Well, the winner caught up with me on his victory lap. At one stage my mathematics marks were negative integers; those were the days of negative marking where they actually deducted marks for wrong answers.

Imagine if they applied that method of marking today; they would have to invent symbols below H in many of our schools. The highest marks I achieved in primary school were for a category on the report card called 'Neatness'.

My music teacher was no help. She approached me one day with what I initially thought was encouragement: 'With your voice, Johnny, you can go far.'

I lapped up the praise, but then came the unforgettable let-down: 'The further the better.'

I hated woodwork because, in Standard 6, everybody had to do this 'practical' subject. I was just not good with my hands. The project for that year was to build an ashtray with some kind of mast in the centre to pick it up, and a half-hollow copper bowl in the middle.

At the end of the year I rushed home and woke up my mother, who was doing night shift later that evening as a nurse in the local hospital.

She was clearly irritated that I broke one of the house rules about night-shift sleep during the day, but damn, I had just completed my design masterpiece.

She rubbed her eyes, saw my white teeth in the dark bedroom, and knew she had to praise my project: 'What a lovely boat, my boy!'

I crushed the bloody ashtray; who needs one in a non-smoking home?

I found my greatest learning outside the classroom. I was the Toweel (the surname of a famous boxing promoter family) of my primary school, organising regular fights after classes between the biggest boy from the Afrikaans class and the equivalent Goliath from the English class. Somehow the Boer–Brit language struggle found its way into my school.

I would set the time and the place and decide the winner. Bloody noses were common. Then one day, without telling the Toweel-wannabe, the two giants decided to turn on the promoter and beat me up for fun. The non-paying crowd collapsed in laughter, and there were no more fights after that.

For the most part, however, my mother made sure I hung out with the right crowd. She would warn us routinely with this hurtful expression: 'I don't want you coming home with every Tom, Dick and Harry!'

My problem was that these were exactly the names of three of my closest friends: Archie Dick, Tom Jardine, and Harry Solomons.

Life was tough under Sarah (my mother's biblical name) who was married to that Old Testament patriarch, Abraham, who together bore a son named Isaac. See-ree-yus. So I went out looking for friends with names like Methuselah, Beelzebub and Epaphroditus.

My dark skin was a mixed blessing at school. On the one hand, I could not prove to my parents that the teacher beat me black and blue; I was black and blue.

On the other, I discovered early that one of the few advantages of being black was that you could not blush. Like the time when a Standard 3 girl I set my sights on suggested I close my eyes for my first kiss ever; when I opened my eyes five minutes later, I was surrounded by a dozen of her girlfriends scattered on the grass, laughing. School was rough, man.

So to all the pupils writing examinations and feeling the pressure of adults on you at this time of the year, I want you to know that school is much more than tests and marks. I want you to enjoy all the other fun things that you experience and that you will remember long after you leave school.

Your teachers mean well, and they genuinely do care about you. Your friends at school will become your friends for life. Your parents obviously want the best for you, even though it doesn't feel like that at the moment.

Most of all, see the funny side of life and of school for, no matter what marks you get, it is not worth hurting yourself over this.

Reconcile our children's future

Children hold the key to a better tomorrow

29 September 2011

As the professor stood before his first-year class at the end of his lecture on the fascinating question, 'Did God really say …?' he suddenly found himself unable to speak.

This module in a new and innovative core curriculum for undergraduates at the University of the Free State was designed to challenge deep beliefs about authority and (any) scripture in fundamentalist societies.

It was an awkward moment for the class of first years as the middle-aged white man started to become very emotional. He could not teach this critical course without admitting his own culpability under apartheid, and asking his racially diverse class of students for forgiveness.

Nobody expected this. A grown man in silent tears. Then, a young black student leaps out of her seat and makes her way to the emotionally distraught professor. She puts her arms around him offering, without words, the acceptance and forgiveness that he sought.

In the same week a strange letter lands on my desk. A black man writes to his new friend, a young white man, on our rural campus in the eastern Free State.

He writes: 'I would like to thank you from the bottom of my heart for the guidance and co-operation you gave us. I thought we were from two different worlds, but with you around it looks like we are the same. You did not even make us feel that you were the boss. We did everything together and you guided us each step of the way, and for that I am grateful.'

A normal letter of gratitude from one colleague to another, until someone tells me that the letter is written to 'Danie', one of the young men involved in the terrible Reitz incident.

How does one deal with the powerful emotions of change as they unfold around you every day? How does one make sense of this countercultural stream of *toenadering* (coming together) as you witness it day in, day out as if the rest of the country is not happening? What do these powerful human encounters tell us about the possibilities for a wounded country? And why is it so difficult for this experience to be taken as normative?

This was the challenge issued by a colleague from another university: 'I do not buy into this project. The images of togetherness are cheesy. I do not believe this is true.'

For a country where violence, insult and abuse represent the norm, of course there is a sense of unease with harmony and conciliation. English institutions immersed in a culture of cynicism pull their noses up at any signs of human warmth and emotion.

There is a second challenge I pick up from angry people on the book circuit: 'This is not the time for togetherness; it is a time for justice. Reconciliation was a mistake; let's take back what belongs to us.'

This is the challenge of the moment: How to turn the peace dividend into a social-justice dividend. The longer we wait in these times of relative peace, on campus and in country, to deal with the mounting inequalities and growing impatience with lack of basic services, the more we risk the human project of togetherness.

The relative quiet following the Luthuli House riots is temporary. We have proven over and over again that we remain prone to explosive anger and retribution. The times of calm must translate into a felt sense of delivery on the needs of the people. Otherwise expect another season of scapegoating in which we blame everyone who is different – the foreign nationals, the oversupply people in the Western Cape, the farmers, the whites, those with Mbeki tendencies (whatever that is) and more.

Behind this lull remains the as-yet unaddressed crisis for the long term: a school system that continues to drop tens of thousands of black youths without hope onto the streets of South Africa. Our short-term interventions to deal with housing or health or social welfare are Band-Aid solutions as the army of poorly educated, jobless youth grow with every year of failed schooling.

The question I get asked most often in book sessions around the country is this: Is there hope for us?

My answer remains the same: 'If the future of the country depended on you older people in the room, we're screwed. But since it depends on your children, I am extremely hopeful.'

Let us give our full support to them as our youth once again attempt the fearsome Senior Certificate examinations which will determine the future careers of so many. And let us be there for them, whatever the outcome.

To party or not to party

What is the role of party politics on university campuses?

22 September 2011

The argument is made, and here I agree, that student politics is a vital component of the transformation of South African universities. A university is, without question, a place that should accommodate and give expression to the range of political ideas and ideals of the broader society. It is a place where such ideas should be articulated, defended and contested without fear. Indeed, student politics is and should be a mechanism through which to learn the habits of democracy and to learn the duty of service to the disadvantaged.

Unfortunately, the debate on the place of student politics in the post-1994 university is often drowned out by the loud and intolerant voices of the demagogues of our society. As a senior politician recently put it, 'You can only reason with those who are reasonable.'

Student politics should never be reduced to party-political activism. Universities enjoy a vibrant student politics that is not, organisationally, a mirror image of what exists in the parliaments or governments of a particular country. This is what party activists want, and this is what represents the real danger to the future of institutions of higher learning.

For a long time tertiary institutions such as the University of the Free State and University of Pretoria organised their student politics exclusively on the basis of political structures in parliament. So the only options for student voting were the DA, ANC, Freedom Front Plus, COPE and the like. Student politics outside of this party-political frame was not accommodated, so thousands of students simply abstained from participation – and that in part explained the low voter turnouts in student elections.

The results were disastrous. The weeks leading to the elections would witness the most racist, provocative and divisive campaigns in which universities would often have to seek relief from posters or campaign speeches besmirching the reputations of people or insulting one or other group simply on the basis of their race. The so-called student parliaments became a platform for racial hatred and race-based vindictiveness that contributed nothing to political insight or the resolution of real problems faced by students. In 2010, such behaviour almost derailed the hard work of student transformation at the University of the Free State.

The public needs to know that university campuses are in danger of becoming little more than recruitment sites for politicians in national and provincial politics.

Senior politicians deploy and fund students who take eight, nine or ten years to complete a degree, doing one module at a time, and failing often, but carrying out their political duty to destabilise academic institutions, if necessary, should they not dominate the campus politics.

Where there is a time limit on a degree, the deployee simply shifts to another undergraduate degree to prolong their time as activists on campus. As they go along, mimicking destructive youth behaviour outside of the campus, they destroy the academic project of the university and they derail the project of building non-racialism within the student body.

A university is not and should not be reduced to an agent of party-political machinery outside the campus. There are already a number of institutions that have lost their essential mandate as places of higher learning through prolonged crises and contestations that have nothing to do with ideas but everything to do with positioning for political parties on the outside, and for the political careers of student leaders with such ambitions.

That said, students should be able to register their political organisations and participate in campus politics. In this respect, the students, academics and ultimately the council of a university decide how student government is organised.

There are at least three options. One option is to organise student elections only on the basis of external party-political referents. Another option is the so-called hybrid model in which students have the choice of either party-political or independent candidates to vote for. A third option is to have students stand as independent candidates on platforms not tied to a political party.

There are positives and negatives associated with each of the options, and some options work better in some universities than others.

To describe any one of these three positions as more or less progressive (or conservative) than the other is disingenuous. It is perfectly possible to have a progressive politics within each of the three models. A university has to decide what works best in its particular institutional context.

The party-political system destroyed race relations at the University of the Free State. It again racialised the student body by forcing students into white or black camps according to the racial dominance of a particular party.

It led to outright conflict, when dominant groups wanted to make a point not through reason and deliberation, but through physical violence and the constant insult of those who looked or believed differently.

It was these on-the-ground facts that led a broad student transformation forum to recommend a policy that organised student government on the basis of independent platforms that could, in any event, be contested by candidates who came from one or other political grouping.

But there was another reason the council accepted this model: it provided for a broader range of student politics beyond what was available in the party-political structure alone. Students from cultural bodies, sports organisations, residence life and so on could all participate in student government without feeling they would be excluded if they did not follow the few party-political structures on offer.

It is this delicate relationship between the autonomy of universities and the interests of external political parties that must be kept in balance.

An open letter to SA's youth

Making sense of the madness

1 September 2011

This must be a very confusing week for you. You saw the children of Cosmos High trying to overturn a police van with school bags still strapped to their backs.

You saw the pupils of Goldfields High ripping into one another with blood streaming from the mouth of one of the fighting girls.

You saw children of your age among the hordes that attacked police and assaulted media workers in central Johannesburg in one of the most violent protests to visit the city in recent times. You can be forgiven for wondering 'what kind of country am I living in?' or, as some of you might have thought, 'how can I get out of this place?'

So I thought I would share some pointers that might help you make sense of this madness, and help you secure your future in this otherwise beautiful country.

- You are not alone. The violent youth do not represent all South African children. They are a minority, so keep perspective. Most of the near-13 million children in our schools are decent. Even though more and more youths think that it is okay to burn, break down and respond violently to things they want or against people they disagree with, always remember that most of our children, middle-class and poor, still believe in things like respect for other people.

There are more good people among us than there are bad people.

- You are not a victim. The worst thing you can do is to think that you are powerless in the face of this social decay in South Africa. Do not be a spectator in the face of this vile conduct among some of our youth.

Write letters to the press or call in to radio shows objecting to the trashing of your city.

Participate in political structures and demand decent public behaviour in politics and everyday life. Mobilise within faith-based communities to set a public standard for social behaviour. But do not simply sit there and condemn the bad things: do something about it.

- You can do things differently. Organise discussions on conflict resolution by inviting activists to your school to talk about alternative means of expressing concern or dissent. Learn how to reason with others in ways that argument trumps anger and reason replaces revolt. Make sure your school has an active debating society where the habits of democracy can be practised; there are more and more inter-school debating competitions that you could participate in. Organise other youths to march for peace and to show how peaceful protests can be more powerful than violent protests.
- You have powerful role models. It would be a mistake to think that the current crop of political leaders represents your teachers and mentors. They do not. When you are faced with spineless leaders who refuse to take a stand in the open against public violence, draw on the many positive role models available to you.

The role models I draw on when I am despondent with our selfish, scared, opportunistic leaders are Lucas Radebe in sport or Mamphele Ramphele in business or Samuel Isaacs in education or Father Andile Mbutye in the faith community or Ela Gandhi in the peace movement. These are the great South Africans – and there are many more – who remind me daily that there are more good leaders than bad ones in this country. Draw inspiration from them.

- You must use your most important asset for fighting back. The low standards of public behaviour have one root cause – poor education. Many of the youth you see running around to destroy property and demean people are the products of a bad education.

I guarantee there are school dropouts among them, and learners who are struggling to pass their grades. In nine out of ten cases a person with bad public behaviour is one who failed to take advantage of the education available to them.

Whatever you do, study hard and pass well (simply passing is no longer good enough) so that there are options available to you through university education and in the job market; and so that you are equipped to make a difference as a competent human being in a broken country.

Finally, as I have said before on these pages, you must learn to stand alone. You might find yourself among pupils who find the destructive behaviour of this past week acceptable, even funny. Stand up, speak out, and make sure you are the difference between South Africa's slide into barbarity and the promise of a better country.

Making tough career choices

Consider all the factors when choosing subjects

25 May 2011

'Hold out both your hands,' says a teacher of young children. 'Fat fingers, you will do Latin. Thin fingers, you will do music.'

The relative recalling this experience after more than three decades speaks with a hint of bitterness about how he missed out on music education. This time of the year the same kind of recklessness is experienced by hundreds of thousands of South African children.

In Grade 9, children – or rather their parents – have to choose their subjects for the last three years of high school. It is not an easy choice, for the subjects you choose during these years will determine what kind of degree you can do at university, and therefore what kind of job you will be qualified to do once you graduate.

Of course it is unfair to impose on such young children the pressures of life-determining subject choices, but that is unfortunately how undergraduate education is structured at the moment. So how should children and parents decide? Here are some guidelines for the parents:

- Let the child make the final decision – if your son wants to do ballet or pre-school teaching, encourage and support him, and get over your misguided sense of what 'real men' do for careers.

- Make mathematics non-negotiable – all careers require the logical processes, basic calculations and reasoning capacities provided by mathematics. Avoid mathematical literacy like the plague; it is government's way of compensating for poor mathematics teaching.
- Half-ignore the teachers – listen to your child's teachers, but not completely. They do not know everything about your child. Teachers often make mistakes in calculating the potential of a child. Teachers are human, and not immune to their own prejudices about children.
- Stress, but not too much – most children will change their minds about degrees and careers, and some only decide once they get to university. In a worst-case scenario, an uncertain student can do two different undergraduate degrees – a BComm and a BA. The upside? They now have more career choices, and they are probably better educated.
- Whatever you do, do not live your missed dreams through your child. The choice of career for your child has nothing to do with you; it is about them. Long after you retire or leave the Earth, your child has to live with these decisions. If they mess up because they made a wrong decision, it is their mess.
- Expose your child to career interests early. If your child motions in the direction of, say, journalism as a career, find her a holiday internship or day visit to a television studio or a newspaper floor to witness how people work. There is nothing like direct exposure to the workplace that can help a young mind evaluate an uncertain decision about careers. Too many South African

children spend their summer and winter vacations in malls and on beaches; get your child to volunteer in a place of work close to their future career interests.

- Assume your child will change work regularly. Your offspring will change jobs more often and work in other countries more frequently than you did. When researching career options for your child, assume that mobility is part of the equation and make your child aware of this.

That is why, if you can afford it, you should give your child the opportunity to travel and see how people work in other climes. Schools that arrange for travel opportunities for children give them a huge head start over those schools that don't.

This raises the question parents often ask me about the desirability or otherwise of a 'gap year'. I used to take a hard line on this matter, also in my own home.

When my matric son told me about his decision to take a gap year, I asked why.

'To find myself,' he answered.

I found a mirror and told him to find himself. If you grew up poor, it is hard to countenance this middle-class frivolity.

Now I think differently. I see the growing maturity of students who come into studies after a year abroad or a stint of voluntary work on a kibbutz.

Helping your child make subject and career choices requires hard work from you. Of course there is an easier methodology: check their fingers.

Know the past to grasp today

Political grandstanding deprives us of opportunities to teach and learn

12 May 2011

What is the difference between the defacing of Archbishop Tutu's statue in East London (2008) and the tearing down of HF Verwoerd's statue in Meyerton (2011)?

Not much, if you think about it (please read the preceding five words again), for it is done by the same sort of people for the same kinds of reasons with the same kinds of consequences. It is done by people who believe that destroying symbols you do not like, or of those whose ideas you disagree with, is an appropriate way of acting in the world. It is the same people who burnt down the office of a principal in a Cape Town township school last week as they disagree with his position that school premises should not be used in school hours for electioneering politics.

To respond to my question with full-throated indignation, that the Arch is good and HF was evil, is to miss the point of the question. Tutu is often slandered by young thugs in politics, and his bust was once defiled after he spoke out against bad behaviour in powerful circles.

To claim that Arch is a good man is incontestable. And to claim that HF was a terrible man, whose racist ideas contributed to the miserable social, economic and educational lives of black people, is self-evident.

So the good versus evil argument is not only medieval sentiment, it is unhelpful in the present. What I am concerned about is our national tendency, against good and bad people, to destroy without thought.

Of course, in the case of the Meyerton debacle, the removal of the statue was pure political opportunism. Not only did that statue of HF exist under both ANC and DA administrations, and nobody cared; there are hundreds of roads and statues and other symbols of terrible people from our apartheid past that today exist peacefully in big cities and small towns of South Africa.

If what led to the removal of HF's statue were deep and considered deliberations in local communities about the meanings and appropriateness of apartheid symbols in and around our municipalities, I for one would take sides on a decision to consign Verwoerdian symbols to the dustbin of history.

But this did not happen. What we saw was political grandstanding on a sickening scale and the loss of another opportunity to teach and to learn about our tragic past. That is what I, as a teacher, lament today: the loss of teaching moments in the political madness that engulfs us.

My main concern therefore about the removal of Verwoerd's statue is this: How do we teach our children, black and white, about the violent past, if we remove all evidence of its existence? To use a wicked parallel, imagine how much more difficult it would be to teach about dinosaurs in the absence of physical evidence of their fossil remains?

Rather than teach about Verwoerd and his place in Meyerton and South African politics, we tear down reminders of his existence as if such destructive acts in and of themselves rid our society of the racism and inequality that he and the system he supported bequeathed to our country. In short, we displace deliberation with destruction, pedagogy with penalty, and engagement with eviction.

There is now a generation of post-apartheid children who know nothing about Verwoerd, except to use his Dutch name as a swear word. They will not learn that there were Verwoerds in more-recent generations that stood against the mad ideologies of this Stellenbosch professor, and joined the ANC. They will never hear of the racial and ideological complexities of his killer, Demetrios Tsafendas. They will not understand why Trevor Manuel's comparison of Jimmy Manyi with HF Verwoerd was so stinging a reminder of how race-essentialist ideas can survive the removal of the bust of an evil man. All these political youths will know is that anything you do not like, good or bad, you destroy.

Given that most of our high school children will leave school without any Senior Certificate qualifications in history, these public spaces where symbols of various kinds stand must be used to teach about the past as a way of understanding the present and anticipating the future.

Public history must not be reduced to tourist history (Apartheid Museum) or nostalgic history (Voortrekker Monument).

Our children must urgently and critically learn about Verwoerd, or else we risk the birth of many more of his spiritual offspring, not all of them white.

Just call me Professor Nanny

A culture of entitlement will destroy our society

5 May 2011

My undergraduate years were the most miserable of my entire life of study.

I did not want to go to the University of the Western Cape (UWC) for two reasons. First, I did not at the time understand a word of formal Afrikaans, and back then the place was for Afrikaans-speakers. Second, I deeply resented that this and other 'bush universities' were set up as ethnic enclaves; and since I did not then nor now regard myself as 'coloured', I was boiling angry that I had no choices.

But there was another reason for my resentment: I lived in Retreat on the other side of the Cape Flats and to get to UWC took me two hours on a good day, three on an average day. I had to walk, take a taxi, jump a train and take a bus going in the direction of Bellville. Most days my parents had no money, and I had to hitchhike on back roads through Philippi. That journey could take four hours or longer, depending on luck.

I often abandoned the trip to university and walked back home when I realised I was going to miss my classes.

It gets worse. My subjects – physics, chemistry, botany and zoology – meant I had late-afternoon and early-evening laboratory sessions and if you lost the last bus going south, you had to launch your tired body for a late-night hitchhiking experience.

I regularly got home after 8 pm, and then had to rise at 4 am the next day for the trek back to Bellville.

One day I scrambled, bleary-eyed, into the early-morning chemistry class taught by one of the most vicious racists UWC had on its payroll, only to be chased out of his class for being two minutes late. The fact that the Mowbray to Bellville bus broke down on the way mattered little to this excuse for an academic, and I sat sobbing outside N22, the large first-year lecture room. This is too hard, I concluded, and bought the *Cape Herald* with my last few cents to look for a job.

I tell this story because my status update on Facebook went 'viral' when I posted this question:

> My students regularly ask that I organise a free shuttle bus service for those finishing classes late. My human instincts are to say yes. But then my academic instincts set in: is the university a nanny institution that not only teaches students but also feeds, clothes, transports and nurses them? What happened to learning independence? What do students lose in learning if we do everything for them?

In a country that places millions of able-bodied people on government grants, I am afraid that many of our universities have become another in a network of nanny institutions.

Having worked and led in several different kinds of South African universities, I know for a fact you will find that we have long taken on parental and social welfare duties that would make us the laughing stock of universities anywhere in the world, including elsewhere in southern Africa. Students 'demand' that we find food for them, help them to purchase clothes, organise transport for them, arrange their tests outside those academic days that break up a potentially even longer weekend, hire cars and give stipends to SRC members and not compel them to attend classes.

I confess that my wife and I, and most of my colleagues, continue to do many of these things for our students for altruistic reasons. But I am beginning to have doubts about doing everything for students. My own children have to work for their monthly allowances. Even if we can afford to support them, they must learn early on the sanctity of work and the rewards of labour.

I would not want any student to live through the misery of my undergraduate student years. But when I look back, those experiences taught me resilience; they forced me to get up again and again to the point where I stood up and said to my chemistry professor and to my circumstances: 'You can fail me, but you cannot break me.'

It made me look for menial work every Saturday and university holiday, including scrubbing oil off a truck company's platform to make a few cents to help my parents.

What I am afraid of is that our students will graduate and still clutch this culture that the world owes them a favour. Such attitudes will destroy our society.

The unbelievable is possible

An image of a better future

23 March 2011

By the previous weekend the alumni had already sent their predictable text messages: 'You can lose all your rugby matches, but not this one.'

It was the annual rugby clash between alternately cousins and arch-enemies, the University of the Free State (UFS) Shimlas against the North West University (NWU) Pukke. The tension was palpable; the grandstand was full. Even the Varsity Cup mascots looked edgy.

The NWU team started strong, taking a commanding lead. Then the UFS team fought back, and took a slender lead. We chewed our way through the short lunch break, and I swear you could have put cockroaches in the meal, nobody would have noticed in the tension-packed rugby box.

By the last ten minutes, the match hung precariously in the balance. NWU fought bravely, launching wave after wave of attack. The visitors would surely score and break the hearts of 30 000 UFS students and staff.

Then it happened. On the attack, NWU spilt the ball backwards. A huge UFS forward rushed through the gap and, like a fast backline player, collected the ball from the ground and lifted his heavy frame towards the try line. The young forward, with a little jig, threw himself over the line and scored, lifting his body to his knees with a fellow player assisting.

But nobody saw the young black woman student on the sidelines defying the rules of rugby (the match was still in progress), and in the excitement of the moment, running onto the field to embrace the young white student.

That image, shown right, will be framed in my mind forever.

In that moment, the woman set aside history and memory, bitterness and bile; this was her man, the Shimlas rugby player. The photograph shows the left hand of the woman on the shoulder of the player, and her right hand in movement towards his head. The young man smiles in return, lapping up the adoring attention.

In this one picture, you find a story of a campus emerging from its moments of racial bridge-building and reconciliation. In another series of pictures, in the media, a story of a country going the other way as the nation reverberates from a spate of public attacks on an ethnic minority group.

If there is one place in South Africa where students can and should unlearn racial thinking about others, it is on the university campus. It is not enough for universities to prepare students for degrees in the discipline without structured interventions that prepare these young people for degrees in life.

Unfortunately, one of two things happen on university campuses today: either campuses reinforce the racism and bitterness of black and white students towards each other, or they completely ignore the troubled knowledge that young people bring with them to higher learning.

There is little in the curriculum in the organisation of social spaces, in the selection of sport codes, and in a compelling example of academic and administrative staff who consciously break down negative racial perceptions of others and recreate positive mental and emotional dispositions towards brothers and sisters.

For example, how many university campuses these past few weeks organised public lectures and open seminars on the racism of Kuli Roberts and Jimmy Manyi – not simply to condemn these racists, but to try to understand what these public provocations mean, where they come from, and what they do to people in a divided country?

A university's role is not simply to react to bad things in a society – there is a place for moral outrage – but to reflect on what happened, and to work against it.

So what appears to be a staged picture of a spontaneous event at a rugby match is actually the outcome of the work of scores of people over hundreds of hours to build a rugby team that is integrated, a rugby audience that is diverse, an appreciation of a perceived 'white man's sport' in the residences, and a broader set of sport codes (including a university contract with Bloemfontein Celtic to build soccer on campus) that are inclusive.

This picture (and there are hundreds of others) is the consequence of taking incoming students from diverse, and sometimes hostile backgrounds, and bringing them into common and constructive educational spaces where they 'unlearn' bitter knowledge and learn what it means to build interracial community.

What happens next in this frozen frame? The beautiful woman student grabs the head of the smiling player and delivers a firm kiss. Now that's the kind of country I am proud to be part of.

Behind the Reitz apology

Working to heal wounds

2 March 2011

The tension was unbearable. This would be the first time since 2007 that the four former students and the five workers would meet face to face, and this at the scene of the tragedy, the university campus. We all knew that Thursday 24 February 2011 would be a long night.

True to custom, the four boys – now huge men – were there on time, waiting. I studied their eyes and their body language. You could feel the nervous tension emanating from their bodies with their reserved handshakes.

So far they had managed to stay out of the public eye, except for the endless replays of the video footage of the entanglement where what appears to be a series of games played by students and workers turned out to be a racist attack on the black staff as a means of protesting racial integration in the campus residences.

But now, after long and complex negotiations between the three parties involved – the university, the former students and the staff – an agreement was reached to settle the matter out of court.

The dinner arranged might or might not happen in Room 16, where family and food awaited the outcome of the drama down the corridor in the rector's seminar room. This seminar room was the site of many difficult dialogues during my 20 months on the campus; it was also the room where the historic meeting between Julius Malema and me took place late in 2009. If that room could talk.

There was a snag. One, then two, of the women workers wanted to first meet alone with one of the boys. This was risky; what if something went wrong, a private confrontation that could demolish months of hard work by the three sides.

When we heard the request it was clear that this was to be a glorious moment. The first woman wanted to meet with the boy whom she knew longest, and whom she expected to defend her dignity among the other boys. She wanted to know how he could let her down. She wanted an explanation before the bigger meeting with all nine participants.

I cannot imagine what pain these two engagements brought, but I remember leaving the room with one of the workers crying. I called the psychologist to join them.

Then the big meeting in that seminar room. I thanked the three groups for coming together of their own volition, and for recognising the limits of legal remedies for complex human problems. Should they come to an agreement, there would be one more hurdle to cross: the public apology the next evening. They should prepare emotionally and spiritually for that intense exposure to a mixed audience of sceptics and supporters, and the searching cameras and lights of the local and international media. Then it would be over, and they could get on with the rest of their lives.

We agree to limit media exposure, given the intense emotions, fragility and vulnerability of the former students and the workers.

I leave the room, and the workers, the former students and the university representative (also to read an apology) are alone. We sit outside, praying. It is quiet, a sense of serious exchange. But when will they finish? It goes on and on and on. We look for food as the night drags on. Is this going to work?

Then, suddenly: bursts of joyous laughter, like that of a mother finding her child after months of anxious searching. I open and close the door; they are standing, but still talking. Finally the door opens from the inside and everybody is smiling. Hugs and greetings all round. It is finished.

We walk into Room 16, where the families are waiting. One of the women grabs the hand of one of the boys as she walks in; 'That's my husband over there, go and greet him.'

There is something here I do not understand. The media images of four white boys instructing and dominating five black workers makes no sense. It is clear throughout that the women, in particular, have absolute control over the boys. They listen when the women speak, and they do what they are told. There is a complexity here that must still be unravelled.

A stark cultural difference is evident in Room 16. The four boys came alone, their families and new wives and girlfriends stayed away; they would have to take this final journey alone.

The workers brought their families, young and old, and it becomes clear that they also wish to speak, to say how they felt about what happened, but especially to welcome the boys into their families.

I feel the goosebumps rise and fall with warm, endearing statements around the table. 'You are still our children, and we love you,' says one of the workers. 'We are so sorry,' says one of the boys, 'and we wish we could have talked much earlier.'

An older woman stands and sings a familiar African song of thanks to God. There are tears. One of the boys adjusts the tie of the black male worker in the video, the one often overlooked in stories that speak only about the women in the Reitz saga. The students sit among the workers, eating together, occasionally leaning against each other as if to remind the other of their new togetherness. The reconciliation is complete.

The wounds remain, but now they will heal faster.

'We realise this is not only about us,' says one of the workers the next evening, 'but about our country.'

A woman of the world – at 11

Intervene early in the emotional lives of children

10 February 2011

The 11-year-old girl sitting across the table from me is as thin as a rake. She is unusually alert and focused for a primary school child, and her eyes reveal a determination that part amuses, part puzzles.

Then she makes her move: 'I have a business proposal for you.'

What? I had seldom seen such courage and confidence from university students. She stares at me, waiting for a reaction, then continues.

Her story is rare. She had just raised R45 000 for poor students to be able to study at university. To raise this kind of money, the little girl from Kimberley had addressed business chambers of serious-looking giants of industry, and launched money-generating commercial projects of her own.

She had just allocated the money for 2011 bursaries and now needed to build her war chest for the next academic year.

Then follows a series of remarkable utterances and, as I hear her speak, I see my dean of students covering his face as tears of joy run down his cheeks.

'How did you become this way?' we ask this child prodigy. 'Oh,' she says, 'I always knew there were problems around us; I just did not realise their scale. That is what got me to act.'

We are still puzzled. Does this kind of insight and compassion come at birth, or is it learnt early on? After all, this girl had only been on the planet for 11 years!

It is clear that her mother, sitting there, is not behind this remarkable act. The young lady contradicts her mother at times in the conversation, and her sister is completely different, more shy and focused on her schoolwork.

The 11-year-old wants to organise a modelling competition on campus and use the income for student bursaries in 2012.

Then, in a moment of excitement, my dean of students makes a vital mistake. 'Good,' he says, 'we can call it The Sune Zaaiman Modelling Competition.'

The young girl of that name is unmoved. She shoots back immediately: 'No, no – the glory must go to God. I do not want my name on the competition.'

I could almost hear the rest of us swallow down the potatoes prepared for lunch. There is silence, as we struggle with our emotions.

I do not know who came up with the handy term 'emotional intelligence', but this young lady has loads of it.

Which brings me to my favourite bugbear: that subject at school called 'Life Orientation'. Is this not what we should be teaching young people? Do not get me wrong; there are thousands of life orientation teachers who take their work very seriously, and have a huge effect on the lives of youngsters. But when I read stories in recent times of schools with scores of girls pregnant, I really wonder whether a high school education speaks to the choices that pupils make and which have life-altering consequences.

What Sune Zaaiman demonstrates is the capacity for self-control, the ability to hold a position, compassion for others and an intimate understanding of her own limitations. Other children her age are consumed in bouts of selfishness and self-absorption.

Zaaiman has graduated from these childish, immature and self-centred behaviours.

Then again, why do we expect the life orientation teacher to be the one vested with sole responsibility for preparing young people to lead a responsible and compassionate life?

Surely, every teacher should be a life orientation teacher? Without such interventions in the lives of young people, we are damned as a country.

The contrast to Sune Zaaiman is the young medical student from the Medical University of SA campus of the University of Limpopo who appeared on the front page of *New Age* on 2 February 2011.

He was wielding a stick and wearing a balaclava while university property was burning in the background. This is the man who one day will do your heart transplant. His emotions are out of control. He has no respect whatsoever for higher learning. He is a coward, unwilling to show his face after the destruction he had just visited on his university campus. His role is not to build, but to destroy.

Neither Zaaiman nor the balaclava-man was born this way. They became that way because of how adults and society shaped them.

What am I saying?

Intervene early in the emotional lives of children – even before they get to school.

We must break the poverty cycle

University funding dilemma

26 January 2011

The middle-aged mother sitting in front of me is a teacher. With a hint of embarrassment, her back straight-up, she slowly pushes her monthly payslip under my eyes.

Her shaking finger directs me to the section 'after deductions'. There is very little money there. With this paltry amount the teacher and mother supports three children at university.

She can barely afford the tuition and registration costs – let alone books, food and transport – for one of the children.

So she made a decision: she would resign from her job as a teacher, which would allow her to withdraw all her pension funds and use this money to financially support her three children at university. My eyes are still on the line reading 'after deductions', wondering if there is a digit missing.

As I listen to the story of this proud, determined but broken woman, I cannot look up. I am scared that if I did, there would be an emotional breakdown from both sides of the table. All her life this modestly dressed, dignified woman toiled in her classroom to provide her family with food and shelter, banking also on retiring with some income in her twilight years.

Now her personal future looks very bleak, but at least she would be able to give her children the chance of obtaining a university degree.

This was the single encounter that forced us to consider free tuition at our university for former UFS students who fell at the final hurdle. If you owe one or two modules for your degree, you can study in that final year for free.

The reason is simple: you need a degree to find a job to pay off your student loan. The longer you are without a job, the more the interest on your debt escalates. It is a vicious cycle for the poor. Without that student obtaining a degree, she cannot earn money to help her parents pay for the other children waiting in line to study for their qualifications.

This once-off amnesty means that whatever you owe the university does not matter if you can successfully complete the outstanding modules for your degree in one year. This offer can be taken up in 2012 by the thousands of UFS students who dropped out in their final year of study anywhere between 2005 and 2010.

South African universities have an obligation to find ways of breaking the cycle of debt and desperation among our poorest students.

Merely denying students' thirst for higher learning because they have no money is a wicked trick played on the children of those who sacrificed much to bring us the freedom we now enjoy.

A routine administrative turn-away by universities to the plight of poverty-stricken families, desperate to send their children to university, is to deny our history and perpetuate inequality.

In this respect President Jacob Zuma must be applauded for his intention to lift the financial burden on third-year students, but he must implement this plan as quickly as possible so that his welcome announcement does not appear to be another electioneering stunt that again disappoints millions of youths desperate for further and higher education.

The real dilemma for South Africa given the millions of students who failed to access higher learning in our democracy because of money is the incalculable loss in human potential.

We will never know what great musicians and mathematicians, poets and architects, teachers and accountants we lost to a country desperate to rebuild itself in the aftermath of that other great potential-killer, apartheid.

The offer of amnesty to individual students of course has its parallel in the fight for debt relief for poor nations; it's the same thing. And as in the case of nations, individual students who are offered such amnesty must prove that they are determined to take advantage of such a once-off opportunity, pass their outstanding courses and obtain the degree. There can be no more excuses.

Back to the mother who wants to withdraw her pension. We worked hard to find her the money to support her three sons, even though our institutional funds were already exhausted. She will continue teaching and keep her pension, and her children will study without worrying about their mother's future after she retires.

Where is our dignity?

Give children the belief that they can achieve

10 January 2013

I am sure she must regret saying it, but it was a disturbing revelation. In an interview with a Sunday paper, our minister of basic education let slip on the real reason government persists with the passing standard of 30% for subjects in the National Senior Certificate. It stays at 30%, she said, to allow 'slow learners' to exit the system with dignity.

My thoughts drifted back in time to great historical figures like Dr John Dube and Dr Abdullah Abdurahman, from a century ago, to more recent intellectuals like Steve Biko and Neville Alexander, and wondered how their restless spirits must be choking when they hear this kind of utterance by an irresponsible and reckless class of politician.

These educated activists all agitated for the black child, and they would say there is no connection between a 30% pass and human dignity. They would argue, no doubt, that providing a high-quality education to the first generation of high school graduates not to live under apartheid was in fact a sacred commitment of that long and costly struggle for freedom.

And then my thoughts turned to a contemporary heroine, an ordinary young woman called Zandile Kwela.

She appeared on television with her mother and they openly shared their mixed emotions. Zandile scored seven subject distinctions in the 2012 National Senior Certificate (NSC) examinations, including mathematics and physical science.

But her mother had no funds to send her to university. In the background offered by the TV shots you saw the rickety shack and you heard there was no electricity; this remarkable young woman from Menzi High School in Umlazi studied by candlelight. It would surely be a severe injustice if this bright student, despite overcoming incredible odds, would be denied higher education because she lacked money.

We sent the message into cyberspace: try to find the contact details for Zandile. Strangers sprang into action and eventually one of my Facebook 'friends' found a set of numbers. I called, congratulated her and introduced myself.

'I have heard of you, professor,' she said, with an elegance of voice that told me she had those other qualities required for success at university: personal confidence and a command of the language of instruction.

'We would like to invite you to study at our university without paying a cent. Are you interested?'

She is packing her bags and I have no doubt she will soon become one of the still too-few black chartered accountants. I am not sure what happens at Menzi High, but there were a few students clutching bunches of distinctions from this school in a poor, unstable township. Those teachers must have worked very hard and the principal must have led from the front.

What I know for sure is that they set the bar high for all their pupils, and they now reap the fruit of their labours. I am absolutely convinced there are tens of thousands of students who failed and passed poorly in the recent NSC examinations who have the same potential as Zandile to achieve distinctions in their school subjects.

To call them 'slow learners' is an insult, for they face two problems: one is poor educational inputs in their 12 years of schooling (poor teaching, lack of textbooks, limited instructional time, and more) and another is the low expectations by the officials serving them. Thirty per cent does not offer dignity; it offers a dead-end street to the children of the poor – no job, no further education, no skills. It is, in fact, a massive indignity being suffered.

Unlike 10 or 15 years ago, from scores of weekly emails and direct feedback in public meetings, I now find that the general public knows very well that we are being shafted by these 30% politicians.

And the Grade 12 pupils know it too.

'I'll take this B-pass,' a young man told his relative the other day, 'but how on earth are these results a B?'

Then there is the story of another young man who wrote to me on Facebook: 'How can they tell me I qualify to study for a Bachelor's degree when I got 49% in mathematics?'

It dawned on him that no serious university would take him without a real pass in maths.

Dignity, says my dictionary, means worthiness and self-regard, a sense of honour. In the South African context it means restoring that which was taken away from black people over centuries – a belief that all of us can achieve, regardless of skin colour.

Pupils aren't the problem

Making a difference in problem schools

31 January 2013

I was expecting a riot. The 75 Grade 12 students found themselves, by cruel circumstances, inside one of the worst schools in the Free State. The government had withdrawn the subsidy of this quasi-private school because of the terrible examination results. The building was a shambles. Teachers came and left on a regular basis, some not receiving pay for months.

When I visited at the end of last year, I stood in shock as boys wearing ties around their heads drifted in and out of the dysfunctional school while uniform-clad couples 'made out' in the streets outside the gates.

Then, standing in the decrepit outbuilding which constituted the school hall and had no chairs, I waited for a long time for the children to calm down.

'You are not the problem,' I told the pupils.

'The teachers, we adults, are the problem; we failed you.'

Silence and shock.

'You have an attitude problem, but that we can sort out in a day or two; but you are not the problem.'

I told them what the University of the Free State could do for them if they committed themselves to succeeding at school.

The children pleaded for a chance to receive a decent education. Then we all left for the Christmas break.

Now, at the start of the year, the Grade 12s are packed into a scruffy room as I return to deliver on the promise. But there was a risk; would they rebel when they heard the terms? I expected the worst.

'So, children, here's the deal. As of Monday coming, your school starts at 7 am sharp, not at 8 am, and finishes at 5 pm, not 2.30 pm.

'I will start the teaching before I go to my other work at the university. Agreed?'

The students applauded warmly as if they had just been given unexpected, expensive gifts. 'Yes, sir, we will be there.' No riot.

'They will not come,' several teachers reassured me, citing all kinds of early morning and evening dangers and a long culture of tardiness on the part of pupils and teachers alike. The next morning at 6.30 am, there were already neatly dressed Grade 12 learners waiting for class. As the steady stream of young people came towards the broken school, they came to greet me by hand before rushing into the now-packed classroom.

Neat white and green uniforms, every hair in place, an urgent desire for learning.

At 7 am sharp, the class starts.

'Today I will teach you comprehension,' I tell the class in a school where only two students got more than 50% for Grade 12 English.

'What does this word comprehension mean?'

All the guesses were wrong in this class where half of them were doing English Home Language. The final examinations were about ten months away.

As the pace of teaching picked up, however, the energy of the class was unbelievable. New vocabularies were being learnt, a tough essay was being analysed, and students lapped up the new knowledge with an enthusiasm I'd never seen before. I was in educational nirvana.

In the evening, I addressed the parents in English while the young principal translated into Sesotho.

These parents were poor, very poor, their eyes dulled by the daily hardships of making ends meet.

I told them about the intensive teaching plan for their children and how they could help. It is the same for all parents: be involved in your child's learning; insist that they spend three hours after school with their books; make sure they arrive by 7 am for their lessons.

'Here is my cellphone number. Call me 24/7 if there is a problem and your child is not learning.'

The joy and appreciation of these unemployed and hard-working parents make the effort worthwhile.

The next morning I bring Sinoxolo Sem to address the class; the young man from a dangerous school in Cape Town who managed to get more than 98% in history.

'Hallllllllooooo,' crooned some of the girls when they saw this triumphant example of a scholar.

'How,' I asked Sem for the sake of my mesmerised Grade 12 English class, 'did you manage to get such high marks in history?'

His answer, of course, made sense: 'I had a very good history teacher.' And then, almost as an aside, his casual follow-up comment also made sense: 'He was from Zimbabwe.'

Perils of macho culture

Are you contributing to a culture of disregard for women?

28 February 2013

Since the age of about 11, I noticed something very strange. It was common then for groups of men working for the Cape Town City Council to be found on street corners digging, or at the back of those large city council lorries with their spades. When a woman passed, I noticed from a distance, they would say something in her direction. Her body would tremble slightly in shock, and the men would laugh.

I have seen such scenes hundreds of times. In the course of time, what was happening became clear: the men were making sexually demeaning comments, or lewd invitations, to the woman passing by. It was the most natural thing in the world – it is what men do.

I thought of this sick phenomenon as the media swept the nation into a frenzy with lurid details of the tragic rape, disembowelment and murder of Anene Booysen in the quiet town of Bredasdorp.

Suddenly, rape reporting was all over newspapers, from girls in their teens to *gogos* in their 90s. Everybody wanted to march somewhere, hold vigils in public or hang the bastards. The frenzy will die down, just as civic energy dissipated after the brutal rape of Valencia Farmer in 1999 and baby Tshepang in 2001.

To change the epidemic of rape in South Africa, we need to change the culture that produces these kinds of men in this kind of society. It starts with how we raise our boys. Take, for example, the socialisation of the rugby boy. The youngster is taught aggression from early on, and encouraged to be physical in his encounter with the opposition. As some competitive bodies are pumped with steroids, physical fights are common – even deadly ones, as in the 2006 death of Rawsonville rugby player Riaan Loots. Fiery nicknames are points of pride: Bees, Baksteen and Bakkies.

Then there is the home, where the son observes how his father treats women, including his wife. The physical abuse of women is common in many South African families. Wherever I have worked, I would see the head of a colleague drop as I asked how she came to have those facial bruises. This is not only a disease of the working classes and the poor – wife-beating is a classless sport. It is, in fact, no different from beating your children. A defenceless child is beaten for being 'naughty' by a stronger adult. That some use the holy scriptures to justify such assault on the young turns my stomach. When you beat a child he learns that, to get his way, using his hands is acceptable.

It was 'an innocent and playful gesture', said one newspaper when the president 'pounced on' the DA parliamentary leader from behind and tickled her neck and shoulders at a cocktail function last year. Precisely. A man lays his hands on a woman's body, and we smile as we accept such behaviour as normative.

It is in these everyday practices of what men do, and are allowed to do, that we establish in our culture the kinds of gender relations that sometimes explode into the terror of rape. I will never forget the recent CNN interview with a former rapist who, when asked why he did it, responded calmly: 'It was not an issue in my community.'

We need to do things differently. First, teach your boy to cry from an early age. Learning to express emotion in a safe and positive way, rather than through aggression and retaliation, goes a long way to healing the woundedness of men in our society. Second, model – as men – the alternate behaviour, especially in a crisis. In the almost 50 years that I knew my father, I can honestly say I did not hear him – ever – raise his voice towards my mother. That, I know, had an enormous influence over my life. Third, speak the language of love. Tell your children you love them. Fourth, reprimand bad male behaviour in public so your children know there is right and wrong.

Let us not fake disgust when a woman is raped.

Let us ask, as men, how we contribute to this culture of disregard for women in our society.

Let's make jobs work

We can't take the education out of work

18 October 2012

Unless it is part of a mandatory anger management course, do not drive along the N12 between Kimberley and Beaufort West; it will drive you nuts. What seems like every 15 minutes, you are forced to stop and wait forever so cars can travel from the other side on the narrow strip of tar road while your side of the national road awaits fixing.

In your boredom, take a look at the three young workers at every stop-go station. One lazily waves a flag to slow you down; another sits chewing gum (you hope) while waiting to move the yellow barrier out of your way when they release you to go; and a third walks aimlessly back and forth across the road.

I watch these three young people and realise how this country delinks work from education; labour from development. The three youngsters are bored stiff. For the whole day, they sit in blazing sun waiting for cars and trucks to come and go while inhaling a steady dose of dangerous exhaust fumes. Yes, they have temporary jobs thanks to the massive roadworks springing up all over the country. Interesting though, how these jobs materialise around party or national election periods; but that is a subject for another day.

At least you have a captive audience of young people. Now imagine if these young people at every stop were taught mathematics as they sat there. They would be required to count the number of cars passing by, and the number of trucks. They would count the number of occupants per stationary vehicle. And they could identify the origins of cars by number plates. That data would be very useful for all kinds of transportation planning purposes.

But, in the meantime, these youths could learn not only maths, but how to use a calculator and complete a self-administered survey questionnaire. They could discuss results and compare traffic flows on weekdays with weekends. In other words, not only would the hands be working, so would the heads.

Imagine an entrepreneur gave all these stations a mobile refrigerator with ice-cold drinks for sale in the Karoo sun. In the 10 or 20 minutes of waiting, the youths could learn how to account for income and expenditure on a balance sheet instead of sitting there waiting.

While a vital cold-drink service was offered in the heat, learning could be taking place.

With the growing number of unemployed youths floating in and out of temporary jobs, and with the increase in the numbers of semi-literate adults who did not finish school – or finished school with weak foundational competencies (writing, reading, calculating, reasoning and so on), we need to make every job count as a simultaneous learning experience.

We do the future of this country no favours by exacting physical labour from workers without asking three questions:

- What are the educational inputs required for this work?
- What are the educational experiences worth organising in this work?
- What are the educational consequences of this work?

There was a time when South Africa had the most noble, inspiring visions for adult education and literacy. We recognised the many who were left out of schooling either because they sacrificed their education during the struggle or they dropped out to work to enable a sibling to continue in school. Now nobody in government talks in these elevated ways about non-school education for adults.

We spend all our time fighting over the crisis in formal education. This loss of focus on the learning needs of working adults as well as unemployed youths and adults is a tragedy.

The three young workers will become unemployed again when the roads are repaired. Then what?

They could either leave those jobs with the kinds of elementary skills and insights learnt on the job, or they could leave only with compromised lungs from car smoke.

This kind of ambition for learning is something I constantly raise with my colleagues. If the workers who work at the university do not leave with more and better education and skills – whether they work for the institution or for contract firms – we would have failed in our duty as a place of learning. This kind of orientation towards building a learning society requires a dramatic shift in the ways employers think about work, especially among those who had little opportunity for formal education.

So if your domestic worker leaves your employ after many years and she is still a domestic, let me be blunt: you are a terrible employer.

This is service overkill

Counting the cost of keeping students in university

4 July 2012

Scissors Ngidi is in the final year of his BA degree. It has cost the family dearly to keep this first-generation university student in higher education.

Scissors often felt the pressure to drop out and start earning money for his single mother, who is also raising five children still in school.

But Scissors soldiered on, achieving averages of 75% and above in his majors, sociology and anthropology.

Despite his heavy workload, Scissors did voluntary service in the surrounding communities of Botshabelo and Heidedal, teaching life skills to high school pupils.

Scissors even offered to work free of charge for the bank that gave him his bursary as a token of his appreciation for their support.

The bank paid him anyway and this money allowed him to finish his studies.

Because of his character, competence and confidence, the bank offered him a job doing research surveys of their clients as soon as he graduated from university.

His university also wanted the talented Scissors to stay on, offering the young man direct access to a Masters in Sociology and a firm promise that he would be appointed as a lecturer upon his graduation.

I meet, teach and lead young people like Scissors every day of my life. I thought of these promising young students when I heard yet another proposal from politicians to make community service programmes compulsory for university graduates.

The story of Scissors highlights the dangers of an otherwise-good idea.

To begin with, extending the time it takes for a student to achieve a degree and therefore full entry into the workplace brings unnecessary hardship on those ready to work.

What we should be talking about is reducing the number of years it takes to obtain a degree in South Africa, including doing away with the antiquated honours degree so that students can directly enter into masters studies after the baccalaureate.

Keeping young people from full employment could be read as a political trick to keep unemployed or unemployable youths out of the marketplace or in jobs forced on the public or private sector at a price.

Making community service compulsory has the further disadvantage of forcing young people to serve rather than invoke the spirit of volunteerism.

True, some youths will discover the value of service if it were made compulsory, but that kind of coercive logic works better with children in primary school than with young adults for whom the persuasion of exemplars among parents and politicians should be the standard of appeal.

That is precisely the problem, of course; what young people witness daily is a predatory elite feeding shamelessly at the public trough, the opposite of what inspires a commitment to community service.

Nor should the state be demanding community service from the youth. It is better to incorporate community service as part of the training for a relevant degree. There are powerful examples of such a strategy in social work, psychology and teaching, to mention only a few.

My two children are now both completing their year of public service; the one is paid, the other not. But what is crystal clear is the academic rigour required to meet the standards set for professional practice. The profession, not the politicians, is in charge of service learning.

What the central prescription of a political party cannot do is add value to the many ways in which students serve communities during their three or more years of formal study.

I have been astounded how young people – at their own cost and sometimes at considerable risk – reach out to the poor and the marginalised through myriad campus-based activities.

Universities should rather be funded to encourage such service alongside what is formally integrated within the qualification structure for a degree.

Young people, all over the world, are idealists who believe they can change the world. The easiest way to kill this idealism is to subject this spirit of service to regulatory mandates by the state.

Of course I want students to do community service. Learning to serve carries deep meaning and adds inestimable value to a formal degree. But the momentum for such service must lie outside of party politics and state bureaucracy.

What should guide community engagement are the professions and campus career services (formally), and student affairs and administration (informally), without extending the academic years of study.

What is being proposed would be an additional financial hardship on Scissors Ngidi; and it might destroy the spirit of volunteerism that society should cultivate.

Dear Jobless Graduate

Why can't I find a job when I have a degree?

21 June 2012

Jobless Graduate writes to me often, posing a question filled with emotion and frustration. 'I have a degree, but I cannot find a job. How do you explain that, professor?'

There is a veiled accusation in the question, something like, 'You are always telling people to study and get an education; well, my parents sacrificed much to send me to university and now, look, I cannot even find a simple job with this qualification.'

JG is male and female, in early to mid-20s, mostly black, from a poor family, and from all nine provinces.

JG has applied for every job available, starting with one that fits the degree that she studied for and then, later, going for any job that could earn her some money.

JG feels frustrated because he is invited to interviews but the companies never call back. He feels he is there simply to make up the numbers; at his lowest points, he believes they need black faces on parade without feeling the need to hire one. After all, they can claim they made the effort.

So JG, here is my message to you.

The reason you fail to get a job has little to do with your degree. It has everything to do with the other things employers look for in a candidate.

To begin with, take a close look at your curriculum vitae. You will notice spelling errors and large gaps between words. You will see that your paragraphs are not always aligned, and that your references at the end are missing information.

Your sloppy CV is one reason that employers decide, there and then, that you would probably make a careless worker.

You will also see that your CV is quite thin. From this important document it is clear that you did nothing else with your life while you were a student.

You did not belong to youth associations, and I do not mean the destructive political ones that go around insulting people and disrupting classes. You were not part of progressive social, cultural and political organisations that sought to make a difference in the lives of poor people.

Your CV makes no reference to voluntary work or holiday occupations. That part-time job at the Spur might have brought in much-needed cash, but volunteering at an Aids hospice or starting up your own youth literacy project or reading club in the township would have shortlisted you for the job.

Then take a look at the marks you took from your transcripts and pasted onto your CV.

Your marks reveal that you concentrated on passing, and so your 40% in mathematical literacy at school, and your 52% in sociology at university, send all the wrong signals, and here I am not even talking about your meaningless 90% in life orientation.

While you were concentrating on passing, other students were focused on excelling; there is a big difference.

I also noticed from your transcript that you repeated anthropology and political science three times each; fat chance of an interview, to be honest.

Now I want you to reflect on your last interview.

The way you walked into the interview room suggested a serious energy deficit. There was no smile, and you looked depressed, with your drooping shoulders. And for heaven's sake, dress properly.

The way you used language was not upbeat, and you made several grammatical errors that the panel members noticed.

You were not prepared, and this showed when one of the panellists asked you what you had found out about their organisation from Google. Your answer was not cool: 'I have not yet met Mr Google.'

I am glad you did not respond when one of the interviewers, out of frustration, mumbled, 'Bring me Jack Daniels.'

And so you see, JG, it is not about showing up with a degree that matters. It is the other stuff they are looking for, the value added to the degree.

You see, unlike political appointments, they are looking for competence, composure and confidence, and evidence of a life well lived. They want proof of an energetic self-starter who filled her leisure time with service to others.

They want an articulate and accomplished employee who can be trusted to represent the organisation well to the outside world.

They regard an investment in a professional CV writer as demonstrating care and concern for the small things that matter.

And by the way, that line on the CV that says 'Criminal Record – None'. Please remove that useless information just in case they do a background check.

Wrong set of values

Teachers need textbooks

27 June 2012

Even as a fresh-faced BSc graduate, I needed three textbooks to prepare my biology lessons. One was given to me by the school, one was borrowed, and another I bought with the meagre salary of an unqualified (no teacher's certificate at the time) teacher.

In preparation for a lesson, I would use one textbook to teach myself how to teach the concept of pH at school level. I would use the second because it contained the simplest experiments to test the acidity or alkalinity of a solution, and the third textbook offered the best test and examination questions at the end of the chapter.

Without the textbooks, I would have been a lousy beginner teacher. This is what makes the textbook debacle in Limpopo nothing short of criminal, since a simple handbook is the only technology our poorest schools will ever have.

In the presence of an unqualified or poorly qualified teacher, a textbook holds the only instructional content that can help teacher and pupil alike.

A good textbook covers the content required; its chapters offer an outline of curriculum scope and teaching sequence for the inexperienced educator; it gives useful hints for in-class exercises and homework assignments.

More than that, a textbook offers basic literacy in the instructional language, which often benefits parents, too, when the book is taken home overnight.

Since circuit and district officials are often not experts in subject matter and the school inspection system is treated as suspect, the textbook is the only reliable, informed, unthreatening infiltrator of the teacher's classroom. Unless, of course, you are in a poor province, where a simple thing like delivering a textbook collapses as a result of official mismanagement on a massive scale.

If a textbook holds such vital importance in the poorest schools of the country, the question, of course, is how officials in politics and bureaucracy can mangle this simplest of deliveries?

The wrong answer to the question is to assume that this is a 'delivery' problem and that questions of corruption, inefficiency and incompetence alone explain this disservice to the poor.

At root, however, this is a values problem, not a delivery problem.

Any country that cares deeply about its children will not, under any circumstances, allow such a catastrophic disruption of learning.

It is, moreover, disrespect for the children of the poor. There would have been riots in Sandton or Durban North or Upper Constantia if the children of the rich had not received their textbooks halfway through the calendar year.

For the political head of education to refuse to resign is just another case of moribund South African politics in which there is no accountability whatsoever for the failure to serve. These, after all, are children of the poor – who cares?

For the same head to call herself the 'mother' of these children is not only inappropriate language – she is not a mother of other people's children, but a public servant. It is also great irony to then say she would not, as a mother, 'abandon' the children. She just did.

Part of the problem lies in the expectation that national government can control what happens in the far reaches of educational services in rural provinces. There is far too much corruption, conniving, conspiracy and contamination of the long service delivery line between ministerial authority in Pretoria and the unfortunate school in rural Limpopo.

Here is a good example of why we should resist the centralist thirst of some in the Jacob Zuma administration. They believe that central power works better than local authority; both spheres of government, in fact, struggle to deliver because they share the same value set in which the children of the poor take a back seat to personal ambition and party-political interests.

Not even an instruction by a court of law could get the textbooks to the schools at a time when high schools are already preparing pupils for the final examination after the winter break. And when the books eventually arrive, the same cycle of non-delivery and growing despondency will repeat itself in the next academic year.

Whether it is nurses demonstrating care and diligence in the service of patients, or home affairs officials delivering official documents to citizens through efficient routines, or trains running on time without passengers hanging out of the doors, all of this reflects not on delivery, but on a value system that needs urgent fixing. This crisis is definitely not about textbooks.

When doubt is good

Students need to be encouraged to draw their own conclusions

7 June 2012

Demonstrating uncertainty and encouraging students to draw their own conclusions is necessary for a youth that has been socialised into dogmas.

One of the memorably dishonest words used by apartheid politicians when under fire from critics was 'categorically'.

With that single word the charge of torture of detainees or military excursions into bordering states or the official incitement of violence in townships was dismissed: 'I categorically deny that.'

What that infuriating word reveals is a much deeper fault line in our democracy – a rigid, unyielding dogmatism that becomes especially aggressive when under threat.

It is not only in politics that this crude attachment to singular truth expresses itself; our religious organisations are steeped in an intimidating fundamentalism about right and wrong. Schools insist on pedagogical routines that discourage doubt, reflection and uncertainty in a facts-driven curriculum. When our first-year students returned from their study-abroad experiences, I asked them what the one difference was between American and South African campuses.

Their answers were consistent: 'In US classrooms students ask questions.' Our incapacity for a reflective doubt was viciously exposed during The Spear saga. The hardline positions were cemented quickly.

Those who refused to bend to the certainties of the masses incited into action by their political masters were to experience the most aggressive intimidation, bullying and outright threats targeting ordinary citizens since 1994.

The editor of a newspaper buckled under political pressure; otherwise-sensible journalists changed their minds in the heat of opposition; and the owner of a gallery apologised feverishly for the offending artwork with the disciplining politician by her side. The artwork must be destroyed on native soil, says the minister of higher education; no, the entire gallery must be destroyed, says his junior party sidekick.

The shift from reasoned arguments about dignity and artistic expression to raucous calls for the destruction of artwork was swift.

Once the emotional link was made to our hurtful history, the space for reason was shut down. It was as if this country never had a vicious history of censorship in which other dignities were suppressed. There should have been reason for pause; extended dialogues on freedoms in tension as we sought to make sense of the challenges offered by The Spear. But where a nation is so cocksure of itself, doubt gives way to danger.

Yet the main lesson of The Spear is the failure of education. Our political conductors took advantage of this, and appealed to the rawest passions of a semi-literate chorus, no doubt sensing opportunistic advantage on offer to a party that fails to deliver on the basic education needs of the poorest among us. It is the cynicism of this political silencing of doubt that should concern us.

A few days later a senior politician made a public call to university leaders for more intellectuals in society, having just driven one of them, the scared artist, into hiding. Here is my concern: there will be more Spears, in a manner of speaking, to challenge our certainties.

The next time round we will be much more fearful to challenge boundaries, to question authority, to express dissent. We will, and should be, scared.

When Harvard president Drew Faust was recently asked what one book she would recommend to students, she chose Kathryn Schulz's *Being Wrong* since 'it advocates doubt as a skill and praises error as the foundation of wisdom', in line with her encouragement to students 'to embrace risk and even failure'.

I would add to that curriculum the movies *Doubt* and *The Lives of Others*. These different media teach complexity and question certainty.

They put a hold on destructive emotions and force us to rethink starting assumptions. How could schools and universities encourage a pedagogy of doubt? Teach using questions rather than assertions.

Encourage curiosity about everyday problems. Show the complexity in what appears to be simple. Take time to draw out different perspectives on what is taken for granted.

Demonstrate uncertainty, even doubt, in your own teaching rather than assume you must know all the answers. Withhold judgement and allow students to draw their own conclusions as you guide them through rival bodies of evidence. And follow that Finnish maxim: less teaching, more learning.

This will take time, and it will be difficult. One teacher doing this will be isolated, but it's a start. University students come to class wanting 'the notes' and insisting on 'the scope of the exams'. Our young people have long been socialised into social and educational dogmas.

The more we change – teachers, parents and priests – the better prepared the next generation will be to reverse our slide into barbarism.

The future lies in young hands

The real pioneers of a new democracy may still come from the youth

31 May 2012

You could see it on their faces. These senior high school students in this poor school had already survived some tough lessons in life. Many were fleeing from the completely dysfunctional schools of the Eastern Cape, believing they would access a relatively better quality of education in Imizamo Yethu; this basic but functional school on the outskirts of George in the southern Cape.

They must have heard about Derick Petersen, the celebrated principal who had turned a failing school into a national success story. Everybody knows about the miracle of the turnaround at this school, and that is why I came all the way from Bloemfontein to recruit their best learners to my university.

A huge pig blocks my entrance into the school. 'This is a first,' I mutter to myself.

The pig takes one look in my direction and moves out of the way, which opens access to the small parking area. A booming voice can be heard in the distance. I discover it is the principal talking to his charges, encouraging and admonishing at the same time. He is present in his school. Everybody looks busy. They want results.

After an invigorating visit to the school, I try to find a number for Helen Zille. She calls back.

'I want to tell you what happened at Imizamo Yethu,' I said.

'I spoke about role models and shared with them stories about Robert Sobukwe and Steve Biko, warning the youth they should look beyond the miserable role models in South African society today.

'I told them we had great role models in the past, and that we could again have great role models in the future if they were prepared to step up to the plate as the next generation of moral leaders.'

Zille listens carefully, and I can sense she wonders why I would call her.

'Well,' I continued, 'I then asked these young people to stand up and tell me about the one person in South Africa they would regard as their role model. And to my utter surprise, a young woman in front faced the class and said boldly: "My role model is Helen Zille." I thought you should know that.'

I, too, was stunned. A poor black teenager in a black school in a tough township hailing a white, middle-class woman from the official opposition was the last thing I expected in this racially torn country.

'Did anybody object or boo?' asks Zille.

'Nobody did,' I replied.

I told the young woman she was the future of our country: 'When more black youths support the DA and more white youths support the ANC, we are in the process of becoming a normal, non-racial society. Thank you for your example.'

It was a wonderful teaching moment and a hopeful sign about our future.

Every now and again I meet pioneers such as the student from Imizamo Yethu. It is the brilliant young black pupil who becomes the first to be head girl of an overwhelmingly white high school. It is the young black boy who competes for a place in a white rugby team because that is where his passion lies, not soccer. It is the white student who chooses to learn an African language to enable her to do social work in the townships away from the certainties of her suburban home.

As The Spear saga raged around the painting of Jacob Zuma, I missed such pioneering leaders who could step into the heat and reconcile the historic pain opened up by artistic depiction and the sacred promise of freedom of expression.

In a country where doubt has never been a virtue, we all fell into absolute, fundamentalist, non-negotiable positions that incited the vandalism that would inevitably follow. Where was the ANC leader who stood up to defend the artist, or the opposition leader who made the case for presidential dignity?

In the absence of reason and reasonableness on the part of our leadership, the stage was set for the usual toyi-toying masses hoping to influence proceedings outside a court of law.

What a terribly sad moment when what was a pedagogical opportunity for dialogue and exchange became a spiteful opportunity to once again call each other names, vandalise a painting, and seek refuge in the law. The real pioneers of a new democracy might still come from the youth.

A woman's world beckons

Where are all the well-educated men?

19 April 2012

We are running out of educated men. This is very serious because it impacts on the kind of futures we stand to inherit. And to be blunt, 'the future is no longer what it used to be', as the saying goes.

A strong and consistent trend has been unfolding under our noses, and nobody's watching.

More women, compared with men, are graduating from high school and from university, with dire sociological consequences for our still-patriarchal society.

Take schools' data, for example. At the end of last year, 230 846 male students wrote the Grade 12 examination and 166 057 of them passed.

Female students, by contrast, delivered 265 244 students into examination rooms and 182 060 passed. This means, of course, that many more girls wrote the exams (34 398) and passed (16 003) than boys did.

Now, given that this is a trend, multiply these numbers over a five-to-ten-year period and the seriousness of the problem begins to hit home.

Attended a university graduation ceremony recently?

Across the disciplines – not only in physiotherapy, teaching and nursing – many more women than men line up to get their degrees. The top performers are women.

The other day I called together all the 2011 matriculants who achieved six As and higher in last year's National Senior Certificate examination. Of the nearly 200 students who showed up, I had enough fingers to count the guys.

Of course we should celebrate the fact that more girls and women do well in schools and universities than before; that is a good thing. But gender equity is not about men dropping out of school and failing to graduate in larger numbers; it is about correcting historical injustices in terms of equity of access to school and university education for women. There are serious social problems and cultural conflicts ahead.

With more women with higher degrees and good jobs than men, this will surely have an impact on marriages. Ralph Banks, a law professor at Stanford, examines this kind of data among African-Americans in his new book, *Is Marriage for White People?*

He found that, as black women made economic and educational progress, black men lagged further behind. So much so that almost twice as many black women graduate from university as black men every year. Many black women then remain unmarried rather than marry men with less money and lower education (from the book's summary on Amazon.com).

So here's the question for South Africa, where these trends seem to be taking a similar trajectory to what is happening in the US: Will well-educated women marry poorly educated men? And if they do, what will be the impact on marital relationships?

South African men have been thoroughly socialised into thinking of themselves as the performers, as the head of the family, as the main if not the only income generator. For centuries in this country, men carried the social and economic status in the family, aided and abetted by scriptural authority: the man is the head of the home and, in some version of the faith, intercedes on their behalf directly with the Almighty. In the church where I had my roots, the women were not allowed to speak in public worship, to this day.

In the future, this will change dramatically. I predict tension and violence in many homes as men struggle to come to terms with their changed status. Many women might choose not to marry, even as they choose to have children. More and more men will remain out of school, on the streets, and in prison – a decidedly unattractive scenario for social stability and family cohesion.

I suspect that, because of this demographic pressure, women and men might marry outside of their primordial affiliations (race, language, religion, country and so on) simply because there are not enough educated men in their traditional social groups. This is not a bad idea at all, given our rigidity around these inherited identities.

Still, I predict problems for men in making this adjustment. In the future I see more and more housefathers (remember housewives?) increasing among that small proportion of men who swallow their pride and adjust to reality. I see competition among the marrying kind for that small group of educated men. I imagine more and more of these emasculated men following their role models into politics, where in this country you need neither a degree nor any limits on your personal appetites.

The department of labour can relax its employment equity targets: women will gradually assume leadership in corporate boardrooms and university senates. The department of correctional services needs to brace itself for a growing intake of men.

No focus without food

We can't let talented youths fall by the wayside

29 March 2012

This email of 6 March had me choking on my breakfast toast: 'You probably do not remember that last year you picked up a girl near Welwitschia [a women's residence on the University of the Free State campus] who was on her way to the shop; you asked her to come with you and told her to choose her own groceries in the mall.

'She came back with a couple of plastic bags. I was surprised because she had gone to Welwitschia to borrow R5 from a friend so that she could buy chicken livers for supper. That was my roommate. Thank you.'

There is no pain worse than student hunger. You are caught between the promise of a degree that will, they say, one day change your life and that of your family, and the pangs of hunger that keep reminding you of much more immediate, instinctual needs that must be met in order to survive.

Do you stay in class or do you drop out and scavenge for basic resources on the streets?

Do you stay on campus, holding on to that promise of a better life, but find the means of making the money that can still the pains of hunger? And if you simply cannot find time for a part-time job between classes, why not just make that money by selling your body or stolen goods?

These are the hard questions that thousands of university students across this country ask themselves every day. The choices are stark.

I remember days like that as a student. Even though my parents always managed to have bread in the house, I recall days away from home when hunger struck. Like the times I sat outside a bakery shop in Montagu with my cousins and simply took in the smells of bread being baked at the back of that *winkel* to at least give us the sensation of taking in fresh slices of *vloerbrood*, as it was called.

It is a horrible pain, made worse in a university, where you are assumed to have one leg up on the ladder to economic well-being.

It is a colourless pain, and some of my African students find it hard to believe there are white and Indian students supported by the university's No Student Hungry campaign. And it is a pain that can determine the life chances of thousands of university students.

As I watched the superbly talented radio personality Redi Tlhabi interview the inspirational Nicky Abdinor at the launch of the campaign, I could see my NSH students' spirits lifted with courage and determination.

Abdinor is a clinical psychologist without arms and with shortened legs who drives a modified car with her shoulders and puts on her impeccable make-up with her toes.

Yet we are all wired differently. To some, another night without food might be the proverbial straw that breaks the camel's back.

To others, desperate measures kick in, such as servicing the sugar-daddies who trawl some of our campuses in search of vulnerable young women. They often leave nothing but devastation in their wake. Unwanted pregnancies are not the worst problem; deadly viruses can find their way into the bloodstream of a hungry youth.

'You want me to have a good academic record to qualify for a food bursary?' asks one of my students.

'The problem is my weak academic record exists precisely because I do not have that food available.'

The young man has a point.

Even well-intentioned bursaries seldom cover all the needs of a desperately poor student for whom not only tuition and accommodation must be covered but basic living expenses as well. And then it is well known that the bursary is also used in part to sustain the broader family. A dedicated food bursary can make a difference to such students.

We can't afford more talented youths with untapped potential falling by the wayside.

Nor can we expect the government to fill all the holes in the net of student support.

The hunger on campuses calls for citizen action. It takes R30 a day to provide one student with a nutritious meal; that comes to R600 a month and R6 000 a year.

The recipients of such bursaries are required to give back to their communities through a service plan that enables others to benefit from the gift they received.

A missed opportunity

Where is the reasoned debate?

23 February 2012

When Agriculture, Forestry and Fisheries Deputy Minister Pieter Mulder last week made the claim in parliament that blacks had no legitimate claim to large tracts of land in South Africa because whites got there ahead of them, he pressed all the right buttons of the black elite.

A seething President Jacob Zuma could hardly contain himself, nor could a sizeable number of media talking heads, as they choked on their cereal the next morning.

Mulder got what he wanted – a momentary place in the spotlight for an insignificant right-wing outfit in the country.

But the responses were all wrong. The provocative use of the word 'Bantu' this side of apartheid was, of course, meant to irritate and provoke; it's like calling African-Americans Negroes today.

His insensitivity to the land question, knowing full well that the ANC leadership has to restrain with difficulty the more radical elements in its ranks on this matter, is of course irresponsible.

And yes, his outrageous reading of history that ignores a European settlement penetrating foreign land could easily make the blood of a black nationalist boil.

The problem is that these are not Mulder's views alone. He speaks for a few million white South Africans who actually believe this nonsense, even if most will never risk saying so in public.

I recently heard a bitter white dean of an established Afrikaans university make exactly the same point to an informed audience that included a current cabinet minister.

So, instead of seizing on this opportunity as a teachable moment for a next generation of especially Afrikaner youth, our apoplectics got in the way – with Mulder and his motley crew no doubt high-fiving each other behind closed doors inside the very parliamentary buildings they once denied the majority.

'You are from Cape Town,' a very wealthy Afrikaner told me recently. 'Why don't you speak up against the Africans taking over everything?'

I knew where he was coming from. I am at least, in part, of Khoisan origins. My people were there originally before Boer and Bantu, to use Mulder's inflammatory labels.

My family should be beating on our collective ethnic chests and claiming original ownership.

I smiled unconvincingly as I struggled to contain my anger at how he framed me, and how he expected me to separate myself from fellow South Africans.

Given that Mulder is not the audience, the president should have taken time to say what one of the world's most respected scholars of Africa shared with me: there is solid archaeological, linguistic, and genetic evidence that Africans populated what became South Africa hundreds, per-

JONATHAN JANSEN

haps thousands, of years or more before Jan van Riebeeck arrived in 1652.

For example, Nigel Worden, in the fifth edition of his *The Making of Modern South Africa*, addresses this claim and refers to African arrivals 10 000 years ago (hunters and gatherers); 2 000 to 3 000 years ago (herders); and 1000 BC to 200 AD (pastoralists).

From William Beinart to Chris Ehret to Cavalli-Sforza, the notion of European settlers arriving in vacant space, before or at the same time as Africans, would today be regarded as a figment of colonial imagination. If the historical evidence was too much to hold the attention of dozy parliamentarians, the president could perhaps have appealed to common sense.

'Come, Pieter, take a drive with me through Stellenbosch, Paarl, Franschhoek and the Steenberg Estate and convince me that simply through duty and dedication, whites secured these most fertile lands, while blacks just happened to find themselves locked inside the tin shacks of Nyanga and those heated ovens called "flats" in Lavender Hill.'

The Prez might pause at this stage and ask the obvious: 'Are you saying, Pieter, that there were no land acts, no forced removals, no white preference areas to give you advantage?

'So what, Pieter? We are here now, together, having to work out how to live on and work the land together. We have to require fairness in land distribution to correct historical wrongs even as we do this in a way that wins the participation of our white brothers and sisters. If we fail to do this, Pieter, meeting the demands of justice and the ideal of inclusiveness, we are all dead. Is that what you want Pieter?'

Instead of reasoned debate and factual correction, Mulder got what he wanted – an angry, inflammatory response. What tens of thousands of watching youths did not get in this exchange was a vital account of history they would also escape in the classroom.

WE NEED TO ACT FOR SERVICE DELIVERY

'Expect poor children to be stranded en masse in the indistinguishable schools we failed to fix.'

The potholes in our politics

My vote will not lead to better service delivery

18 May 2011

You cannot drive straight along the road into Kroonstad. The stretch of tar that connects the N1 highway to the other side of town, where two historic schools named by the colour of their roofs stand, is broken up by large and small potholes.

'There are more potholes in your town than people,' I tell the children of Die Rooidak Skool (*Rooies*) and, later that morning, to the children of Die Bloudak Skool (*Bloues*), to raucous laughter from both sides of the street.

If you want to understand why I did not vote yesterday you will find all the answers on the road from the national highway to these two high schools in Kroonstad. We drive slowly, for if you hit one of those giant potholes you are looking at thousands of rand damage to your vehicle's underbelly.

'You might even drop down one of them potholes and land in Australia, down under,' I tease the pupils still shaking with laughter.

Moving gingerly along the broken road through the town one is greeted by the sight of loads and loads of rubbish along the sides of the road, where once was a pavement. I watched the commuters going to work in these early hours of 17 May and noticed how they dodged the filth, sometimes kicking the dirt on the street, as they made their way through the muck.

Then the surprise. Just above the mounds of dirt there are five, six, seven posters of rival political parties urging the filth dodgers and the pothole avoiders to vote for them.

The largest posters on display belong to the party that rules in the town. The word 'audacity' comes to mind.

'There is no shame,' I tell my driver colleague. I would run and hide if I had messed up this once-beautiful town in the northern Free State, not put up my posters asking for another opportunity to run the place into the ground.

'Scandalous,' I think to myself.

Why run for office, again, if you messed up the town? It's quite simple, really. The locals tell of a recent scandal of people in the municipality caught out buying furniture for their offices to the tune of R95 000 for a table and excessive amounts to adorn their work spaces. This is why people engage in violent conflict to get on election lists. It is not to make sure the dirt is collected or the potholes fixed. It is the only way to gain access to and raid the public coffers for personal enrichment and outlandish greed.

Which brings me to the greatest mystery of all – the simple fact that the party ruling in this town will be returned to power by a majority vote by the very people underserved and exploited by their local rulers.

Why? Because most of us still vote our skins and many of us still vote our memories. We are still resolutely tribal in our affiliations.

To be sure, there are signs that some municipalities will change hands in favour of those who actually make a difference in the lives of local people. In this respect, says a good friend, there are interesting calculations being made by the poor, like: 'I will vote DA locally for delivery in my municipality and ANC nationally for history in my country.' I am not sure if the results will show this reasoning constitutes a national trend.

That is why I will not vote. My vote is meaningless in these contexts. It will not change the character of leadership at the local level. It will not lead to better service delivery to our people or more respect for fellow citizens. It will be overwhelmed by the millions who vote based on ethnic loyalties and apartheid memories.

I was rebuked when I declared at the recent Franschhoek Literary Festival that I would not be encouraging people to vote. I waited all my life to vote. But we are in danger of making a serious mistake when we reduce democracy to the act of voting. I will be fighting for democracy, for sure, every time the powerful try to muzzle the media.

I will be out there encouraging democratic behaviour daily in the schools and universities of our country.

But until my vote can reasonably stand a chance of replacing the arrogant ruler with the genuine public servant, I will stay indoors and keep myself warm on this frosty Free State morning.

Ruling courts disaster

Legal intervention into the future of our schools

15 December 2011

You would be forgiven if you thought Boissie Mbha was a centre back for Pirates or the fifth member of the kwaito group Big Nuz.

Until last week few people outside the legal fraternity would have heard of the judge who, in a single verdict, might just have completely recast the future of schools in South Africa.

In a classic tussle between a provincial department of education and a school governing body, the province demanded that the school enrol a pupil despite the governing body's insistence that it was full.

Nothing odd about that until you realise the school was a former white institution and the child was black. This being South Africa, all the ghosts of the past came back visiting with a vengeance.

I promise you if the school and child were black, or both were white, there would be nothing to write about.

Judge Mbha sided with the government in a series of pronouncements that make no sense to me. This was about the right to basic education, he reasoned.

I am not sure how a child attempting to transfer from the Lifestyle Montessori School to another school constitutes the denial of basic education. The judge then goes on a lengthy diatribe against the protection of white privilege. This too makes no sense when the school already enrols 388 black pupils of whom 52 (of 120) are in Grade 1; in other words, the school is closing in on 50% black enrolment and will, no doubt, become a dominant black school in time. How does this preserve racial privilege?

The judge then queries the link between admission policies and school capacity. But surely a central tenet of admission policy is to ensure classrooms have manageable numbers that teachers can cope with? That is a pedagogical matter to be decided by educators, not a legal matter to be decided by a judge.

To imply that government bureaucrats determine school capacity raises an even more fundamental question: the right of parents to decide on a simple school matter like how many children it can manage.

Here's the rub. The department of education has not accounted for the fact that more and more township schools are running on empty because of dereliction of duty by provincial government to provide high-quality education to all our children, where they live. In response, poor parents understandably move their children, at great cost and risk (dangerous public transport), to suburban schools, most of which can no longer be described as white by enrolment.

What makes this judgment even more puzzling is that the parents at the second school themselves built nine additional classrooms and out of their own pockets paid for additional teachers simply to ensure that the education of children – including 388 black pupils – did not succumb to the serious dereliction of duty by the department of education to fix its broken schools where, as we know from research, most children cannot read or write or reason at the grade level.

So what does the judge do? He sides with the politicians and the bureaucrats to make sure no schools work rather than protect the few that do – mostly on private monies.

I have seen throughout our country how former white schools became all-black by enrolment, with 50 or more children in a classroom because of incompetent management by the provincial government – not because there are black pupils inside of them.

There are very few former white public schools that remain predominantly white, and it is simply a matter of time before all our schools are majority black. In the meantime, we would have stripped parents of their already limited say over school policies and we would have reduced the entire school system to a massive mess of mediocrity.

I have seen this movie before in post-colonial Africa, with familiar actors in the moving rhetoric of a narrow African nationalism in which Judge Mbha so eagerly participates.

This is no longer about race; it is and will increasingly be about class. A recent study in the US shows that in countries with a similar history of racialised schooling and capitalist education, the achievement gap between the well-off and the poor becomes greater over time than the gap between black and white.

Expect the middle classes to move their children into private schooling if a higher court does not reverse this disastrous decision. Expect poor children to be stranded en masse in the indistinguishable schools we failed to fix. And guess where the politicians' children will be sitting.

No hope for teachers

Will teachers get smarter if we test them again?

13 October 2011

So, yet another report tells the sad story that many of our primary school teachers cannot do simple fractions. We know this, of course, from so many other research reports over the years, such as the recent Annual National Assessments on Numeracy and countless international studies of achievement in mathematics among South African pupils.

We know this, and I asked myself the other day: What purpose does it serve to say the obvious over and over again? Will teachers get smarter if we test them again and again? Will pupils get a better deal in maths classrooms if we expose the fraud that passes as education for poor children? Of course not.

So why do we keep doing this? I suspect it is out of frustration with the incapacity of our government to come up with game-breaking solutions to the crisis. We hope that some provincial head of education will be struck by the serious lack of subject matter knowledge in mathematics and come up with a smart-bomb equivalent for effective teaching of the subject. We pray that our minister of basic education will appear among the fanfare of announcing matric results and put a credible national plan on the table that changes maths learning.

But none of this is going to happen, in part because I suspect that, if you gave those simple fractions tests to all the officials in the national and provincial departments of education, you might get the same startling results. Try me on this one.

There are two serious reasons why our government will not react to this latest data on teacher achievement, or more accurately, underachievement, in primary mathematics. First, it does not care enough. There is simply not enough concern for the poorest among us. After all, who cares when one's own children are in fancy schools where teachers can, in fact, do fractions?

I see a lot of political grandstanding and official pretence, but I have not seen in any province the kind of educational leadership that rolls up its sleeves and immerses senior politicians and their key strategists in the poorest schools to change the mathematical life chances of pupils. You are more likely to find these politicians and senior officials at branch meetings of their parties plotting their political survival than in the trenches making sure teachers receive the training and support they need to overcome knowledge deficits in mathematics.

What really gets my goat is how the same politicians who fail to act on the crisis in foundational learning then criticise universities for entry standards that, in their calculation, 'keep out poor black students' because of low marks in subjects like mathematics.

In other words, universities are supposed to participate in this fraud called education by extending the mediocrity into higher learning. Sadly, there are university leaders who do this without conscience, thereby ensuring that the black youth receive a microwaved version of Bantu education all over again. Verwoerd must be smiling in his grave.

Of course universities have a responsibility to provide bridges to higher learning for young people failed by the school system; our apartheid history – if not also our post-apartheid incompetence – demands such responsibility.

At my own institution, the University of the Free State, we provide three different ways into university for those who do poorly in school maths and other subjects; as a result, we have produced thousands of teachers, doctors, chemists and other specialists.

But you do not ask universities to lower the required standard for admission into the mainstream of higher education; that kind of mindlessness would serve the short-term political ambitions of a few, but it would put the final nail in the coffin of higher education in this country. In other words, complete systemic collapse.

But there is a second reason our political heads and their so-called 'technical departments of education' (so-called because our bureaucrats are too often political deployees bereft of the educational knowledge required to change schools) will not respond to teacher underachievement – they simply do not know enough themselves. One of the most incompetent decisions of the politicians was to give teachers pre-planned materials for teaching, official confirmation that teachers knew too little to be trusted.

Instead of effective intervention on teacher knowledge, we Band-Aided the problem.

So what do we do in a country in which the people responsible for systemic change in schools do not care enough and do not know enough?

When the tail wags the dog

Where is the authority in education?

6 October 2011

It was one of the most disturbing images I had ever seen.

On the inside pages of a major newspaper last week, a photograph is shown of a principal running away from his pupils at Chris Hani Secondary School in Khayelitsha, Cape Town.

The bespectacled principal looks young, perhaps in his 30s, and is definitely a man who thinks about matching clothes when he dresses for school every morning. But today the neatly dressed man is clearly running, and behind him Grade 12 pupils appear to be throwing things at him. It's a painful sight, a principal running for his life, with laughing pupils behind him.

The photograph represents so powerfully what is wrong with our schools – the complete loss of authority in education. The roots of this problem lie way back in the early days of our democracy. We inherited a 'flat democracy' in which everybody decides about everything. The reaction to apartheid's iron fist was to make people pretend that we all decide about detail, and that there was no authority that could take the lead in decisions without everyone participating. This flat democracy took on farcical dimensions in the early years of our new government when right-wingers, racists and arch-conservative groupings were made to believe that their opinions on the interim Constitution would count for something. The boxes of written commentary came rolling into parliament.

The people would govern.

I actually like this version of democracy. I thrive on the idea that people buy into a new plan or new policy. There is a deep sense of fulfilment when everyone in a company or community goes along with a new strategy. The chances of sustaining new leadership initiatives are greatly enhanced when there is broad support for that change.

Taken too far, though, what does this mean for leadership? What does flat democracy mean when leaders are so fearful of their followers that they are afraid to take a public stand? What if what the followers want is wrong or unethical? What if the leader's survival depends on the support of the followers, and she behaves accordingly? What if the followers believe they can violently attack or overthrow the leader since they put him there? What if the followers are like their leaders?

This is the dilemma of our democracy at the moment. Our political leaders are so fearful of their followers, including fellow leaders, that they find it difficult to discipline them early or firmly – which explains the rot in politics from the Union Buildings to the municipalities. And there is good evidence of what happens when leaders try to discipline their deputies – they get recalled to the position of former president.

This is what happened at Chris Hani Secondary School – irrespective of what caused the attack by security guards on a pupil, the apparent spark of the protest.

Our pupils believe they can decide on the fate of a principal and defy any authority to run a school. Our unions sometimes meddle in the appointment of teachers, caring more about advancing comrades than ensuring competence.

Our students regularly fight university authorities across the land because they believe they can decide on catering and residence tenders.

Our councils on some campuses hold academic decisions hostage, not understanding that their roles are restricted to governance.

Some senates are loaded with non-academics, in the name of flat democracy, turning this academic body into a political circus with no capacity to adjudicate on research, teaching and learning. And that is why every year there are two or more universities run by ministerially appointed administrators.

To get our schools functioning again we need to be clear about different roles in our democracy. Teachers teach, pupils learn, governing bodies govern, unions advance the profession and protect their members from abuse, and education department officials finance and support the schools.

For this to happen, we need to give our leaders, the principals and their teams, the sacred authority to lead sensitively but firmly without fear of other actors crossing the lines of responsibility assigned to them.

And when a principal fails in their duty to lead, there are mechanisms for relieving that principal from duty – starting with the governing body and then the provincial department of education.

If this lawlessness in education continues, the youth become used to wrecking the lives of leaders, undermining teaching and learning, and capsizing the project of democracy which is still very much under construction.

Lethargic leadership to blame

The emotive and political value of the word 'ungovernable'

25 August 2011

Some words outlive their sell-by date without the user even knowing it. One such tag is the word 'ungovernable', claimed to be issued recently, like a fatwa, by the head of the National Youth Development Agency.

It is most often used as a threat by those who were either children or still unborn during the 1980s, when the word first surfaced in political rhetoric during the most difficult days of the anti-apartheid struggle. It was used as a weapon of war against an illegitimate government; it was as much a tool to mobilise the masses as it was a signal of disregard for white governance in a largely black country.

It made a lot of sense then, but those with an audience now have moved on to other sneaky terms like 'black snakes in the grass' (at least the snake is black, some say).

But the word 'ungovernable' has retained its emotive and political value. For that reason every now and again some protesting group or mindless demagogue would retrieve the word from recent memory and threaten to make a democratic state 'ungovernable'.

That is impossible: the people and their representatives (whether we like them or not) govern, and while some mob might shut down some essential service for a while, that hardly counts as making a whole country ungovernable, as was the original meaning.

Still, the images of striking workers overturning rubbish bins, burning trash, robbing street traders and assaulting non-striking staff evoke images of ungovernability from another time.

The fact that this happens almost as if on schedule year after year gives the impression that government has no effective answer to this routine trashing of public spaces.

We briefly observe and express disgust, and then move on to other things as if this public display of indecency is the most normal thing in the world. We certainly do not believe that the government is going to collapse as a result; they will be back next year.

And that is precisely my concern. What happens in a society where public indecency becomes normative? What does it say about us as South Africans when the public slander of commentators and the public trashing of cities become such an everyday event that nobody notices? What have we become when the provocation of ungovernability does not evoke the necessary political response from our leaders?

I have considerable respect for deputy president of our country, Kgalema Motlanthe; he is a decent man. But I was puzzled by his call for ethics to be taught in our schools. That is probably a good idea in a normal society. The problem here is that they are already being taught ethics – by their political elders. When they read in the media one story after another about corruption, they are learning ethics. When they see their parents and siblings trashing the streets of our major cities, they are learning ethics.

When they see youth leaders besmirching the reputations of leaders of this and other countries, you better believe the children are learning ethics.

You cannot inject ethics into children by preaching it through the school curriculum, no more than an alcoholic parent can effectively teach an observing child about the dangers of substance abuse. The more powerful curriculum is what children learn about values through everyday observation.

When riotous youths pillaged the shops and destroyed vehicles in major cities in the United Kingdom, starting in north London, the British prime minister returned from his vacation and walked into the middle of a street outside his residence to condemn what went wrong, and to announce what would be done to correct the social delinquency on display in the streets of his country.

When the same kinds of public violence were executed by the South African Municipal Workers Union strikers, not a whimper was heard from our leaders.

What will be the consequences? It will happen again and again. No matter what agreements are made this year between the negotiating parties, expect this annual pillaging of our cities to continue next year and the year after that for one simple reason: the lack of, the failure of, leadership.

Schools are not places that lead the change in their surrounding communities. They tend to more often reflect the rot in society. In the words of one brand of educational theorists, schools are more likely to 'reproduce' the existing order than they are to transform it. The answer to the rot lies outside of the schools.

When will we be enlightened?

When more whites vote for the ANC, and more blacks for the DA

1 June 2011

I am not a minority. I am part of a majority that cares about decency in politics, about freedom in the media, and about quality education in our schools.

The word 'minority' is imported from the US, where it is used to describe those who are not white, as opposed to the majority; that is, those who dominate and will continue to dominate economics, politics and society in that country for some time.

It is a dangerous word in South Africa. Here we are in the business of building a common identity as citizens of a new country, where we will no longer refer to each other by skin colour or demographic count, but by allegiance to higher values and commitments.

There is another reason to run from the word 'minority'; it is a term imbued with apartheid meanings, where 'minority' was once a sympathy card to explain why whites needed to stay in power at the risk of being 'overrun' by a black majority. Now, after the elections, the word is in vogue again. This is not good.

The word makes its unwelcome return because 'majorities' have a problem explaining why 'non-Africans' vote for other parties like the DA. It does not occur to the uncritical users of the term that small but growing numbers of African voters vote for parties other than the 'African' National Congress. Nor does it fall within the reasoning of politicians and the media that 'minorities' who now vote for other parties once voted for the party that wins the majority vote.

What these shifts suggest is that voting patterns have little to do with 'majorities' versus 'minorities' and everything to do with what the dominant and opposing parties project as their core values in theory and in practice.

If majority politicians (1) had not made racist comments about the oversupply of coloured voters in the Western Cape; or (2) did not sing 'Kill the Boer' to entertain 'majority' crowds; or (3) did not only appoint 'majorities' in every election to the two most powerful positions in government (leaving out the sop to FW de Klerk in the first round); or (4) did not describe the problems of education as 'the problem of the African child' but of poor children everywhere; or (5) did not racialise critical commentary into majority versus minority (that is, the backward, counter-revolutionary, racist, to name a few) opinion, we might very well have seen a different election result in terms of who voted for whom.

In short, our public discourse in the years and months leading up to the election created minorities at the very time where we needed to build a strong sense of solidarity across apartheid's fault lines of race, religion, ethnicity, class and gender.

All political parties play this silly game. It is very important that 'Africans' run for and attain positions of power in the Western Cape, for example, and that non-Zulus contest and win power in KwaZulu-Natal. Tony Ehrenreich and Patricia de Lille are both people I respect deeply, but it is cynical in the extreme to think that so-called coloureds contesting for mayor is the only way people in that part of the country would consider voting.

What people want is decent leaders of any colour. They want consistency of service between elections. They want an uplifting language that does not put the fear of retribution back into the minds of the defeated – 'We will take their land', for example. They do not want threatening and demeaning words to describe black people who think differently from the 'majority', for that means anyone can come under attack for not thinking like 'majorities'.

To be sure, there is a core of people in this country who will always vote tribe or race no matter what happens to their personal circumstances – but that group of people is a minority.

With every passing year, I sense that primordial loyalties matter less and less for most South Africans. The day more white people vote for the ANC and more black people vote for the DA, the more we become an enlightened democracy, where ideas trump skin. We are getting there, slowly.

One way to accelerate that movement towards a culture of democratic practice is if political parties refuse to play the race or ethnic card to obtain advantage. But we can begin by changing the way our language accounts for the social realities around us.

Education's date with bad fate

If this doesn't frighten you, nothing will

13 April 2011

There is a nasty story doing the rounds about a dedicated teacher who died and arrived at the Pearly Gates, to be offered a tour of the various mansions in heaven.

She saw a block of the most beautiful mansions, and the archangel confirmed that the noisy guys in white coats were doctors living there because of their dedicated service to humankind. Around the corner the newly arrived teacher saw an even more impressive block of mansions.

'That's where the social workers live,' said the heavenly host, 'because of their selfless sacrifice to humanity.' The rowdy social workers waved to the incoming teacher through the wide, open windows.

Down the road were the most astounding mansions possible, and this was where the teachers were located.

'They did so much for generations of children,' said the angel, 'so they get the best accommodation.' But the place was very quiet, so the puzzled teacher asked the obvious question: 'Okay, but where are the teachers?' The angel responded: 'They're in hell, attending a Sadtu meeting.'

Last week one of my best friends died; a devoted teacher and teacher educator named Carol van der Westhuizen.

She was the last of a breed; a teacher who worked through the night to ensure that her student teachers at the University of Pretoria were placed with the best mentor teachers in our best schools. She was the pioneer who persuaded our student teachers to practise in schools different from the ones in which they were taught.

She satisfied all the criteria for what we call a professional in our craft: that dedicated person with specialist knowledge who sets and even exceeds the high standards of her profession. She was both teacher and scholar, someone who reflected deeply on her work in order to improve it, and from these reflections published her research in leading journals in the world.

The fact that Carol came from a teacher's college that had closed down did not prevent her from making that difficult transition from college educator to university scholar. She must be in one of those mansions worrying, no doubt, about the hell she left behind in our school system.

Which brings me to the historic conference, held last week in Soweto, to address the now-permanent crisis in the schools of the township.

The irony would not be lost on those who attended Crisis Committee conferences in the same place in the 1980s to discuss the education chaos in township and country. That was under apartheid. Four governments and five presidents later, we are still there discussing the same crisis in the same place. Makes you think, doesn't it?

What really moved me, though, was the voice of Sibongile Nthiyane, a beautiful young learner in her final year of high school. With a poise and courage that you seldom see among our youth, her speech to the Soweto audience of parents and teachers included the following scary excerpt:

> They [that is, her teachers] come to school drunk, never dressed properly. They never come on time. They know they are paid to teach us, but we have to beg them to come to classes.
>
> They send us to buy alcohol during school hours; which they drink during school hours.
>
> These so-called parents of ours are the ones who tend to date us these days; how can you stand in front of me and teach me, when you know you are dating me?

If this does not frighten you, nothing will. No wonder parents and teachers in Soweto taxi their children to the leafy suburbs of Johannesburg, causing the closure of several schools in this area.

What Sibongile is drawing attention to is a complex and corrupting school culture that has long destroyed professional routines of teaching and learning among the most vulnerable schools in our country. This can't be fixed with opportunistic political speeches in an election year or by occasional fits of moral pique.

What you have in Soweto schools – and elsewhere – is something so deeply rotten that it will require strong and sustained intervention across this large subsystem of South African schools.

This is something so crucial for politicians to understand, for they work in short-term, election-cycle thinking to secure their positions; and it is very important for provincial bureaucrats to grasp, since most work with limited knowledge and insight into the nature of this school- and classroom-level crisis.

Strike a careful balance

Teachers should retain the right to strike

7 February 2013

The reported efforts by the ruling party to push for education as 'an essential service' might seem, on the face of it, to be a good idea but, if implemented, could further erode the democratic rights available to working citizens.

This is, after all, the party of the secrecy bills and the toxic new higher education laws which threaten to asphyxiate individuals and institutions alike by depriving them of the democratic air that our society needs to breathe the promise of freedom.

These attempts to wield power recklessly and to control on the basis of electoral majorities constitute a much graver danger to the country.

My gut, of course, tells me that government should clamp down on teacher strikes, given the enormous damage done to the education of young children. The protracted strikes in the Eastern Cape, for example, explain in large part the persistently low scores of learners in primary schools (the ANA, or Annual National Assessments data) and in high schools (the National Senior Certificate results).

While the Bill of Rights guarantees the right of workers to strike, the Constitution also holds that '[a] child's best interest is of paramount importance in every matter concerning the child'.

Given that the overwhelming majority of our children come from poor families, it makes sense that this one route out of poverty – a good education – should not be blocked because of strikes by educators whose children tend to be placed in middle-class schools, where there is little or no strike action in any year.

But think again. Imagine you are a teacher in the Eastern Cape, one of the more devoted educators, and you show up day after day teaching your eight or nine classes without fail, only to find at the end of the month that you are not paid because of administrative chaos in Bhisho.

You write letters and receive no reply. You stand in long queues at the district and head offices, only to be told they cannot find your file.

Imagine there are hundreds, or even thousands, of you. The next month comes, and the next, and still no salary cheque. Debt collectors threaten you. But still you show up daily to teach every class with energy and enthusiasm.

You borrow money for petrol or taxi fare just to get to school. It is embarrassing because teaching is supposed to be a proud profession. Then one day you realise the only way to get the attention of your employers is to withhold the only thing you have left to bargain with – your labour.

There are many variations on this theme of distress among good teachers. There are the Grade 1 classes with more than a hundred children in a class and whole grades missing textbooks, as we saw last year.

I exclude the sizeable number of thugs who parade as teachers and those who do not teach, even on the days when there is no strike at all. My attention, for now, is on the good teachers who struggle to do their work and whose complaints are not heard by the officious, cold-hearted brutes in some of the provincial education departments.

In other words, clamping down on teacher strikes would, consequentially, protect incompetence in those provincial education departments who treat their hard-working educators with contempt.

Rather than take away the constitutional right of an employee to strike, we should be talking about the conditions under which strike action should be undertaken.

South Africa's problem is not strikes; it is the lack of constraint and the destruction of lives, property and reputations that inevitably flow from the ways in which strikes are conducted.

Strikes should be a last resort following clear evidence of inaction on the part of the government. Strikes should be limited to a set number of days, and preferably outside of normal instructional time.

Strikes that affect actual teaching and learning time should be made up immediately so the learner is not disadvantaged.

Strikes that are violent and destructive must lead to action against renegade teachers, including expulsion from the profession.

Strikes should under no circumstances lead to intimidation of those who, on the basis of conscience, choose to continue teaching.

And strike participants must not be allowed to disrupt the schools of the poor if their own children are ensconced in non-striking schools; that is unfair.

Sin of consenting adults

How can these teachers go any slower?

2 February 2012

How do you declare a 'go-slow' among teachers in a province that has been on a perpetual 'go-slow' for decades? Did they mean 'go-slower'?

To understand the callousness of our politicians and unionists towards children, and the deep disregard for learning in our nation's schools, take a hard look at the criminal behaviour of consenting adults in the Eastern Cape.

If the apartheid government did to Eastern Cape schools what the unions are doing to them at the moment, there would have been tyres burning in the streets and protest marches through East London and Port Elizabeth.

Yet, it is completely acceptable when black people ruin the lives of black children. Let me be blunt: what is happening in the Eastern Cape is nothing less than disgraceful.

It is not the fact that the province has had more members of the executive council and directors-general of education since 1994 than several provinces combined. It is not that the province suffers from a level of official lethargy and indifference that has become the butt of jokes.

It is not that the province still has ghost teachers and incompetent educators.

It is not that thousands of teachers, often without qualifications, are being laid off. It is not that there are massively overcrowded classrooms and rickety school buildings that have not benefited from investments from the Treasury.

It is, quite simply, that adults do not give a damn about children.

The South African Democratic Teachers Union has a point: the province is incapable of doing simple things right in the way it treats teachers.

The provincial authorities are correct, too: the teachers' union has been a major stumbling block in the delivery of quality education to the poor. A curse on both their houses for, in the end, the children suffer, as results show year after year.

Consider the facts. This, we all know, is the province with the lowest matric pass rate in the country and the only region to experience a decline in the 2011 pass rate.

Even with the National Senior Certificate's ridiculously low pass requirements, the Eastern Cape saw its results drop in 2011 for life sciences, history, geography, accounting and, of course, mathematics. Whole districts – such as Libode, where more than 60% of children failed this high-stakes exam – have collapsed.

Let's take the gold standard for measuring education attainment in a large school system – maths. Every year, fewer and fewer children write maths.

There is a reason for this – the forced migration to the infinitely easier mathematical literacy. Even with this face-saving manoeuvre, only 7 469 of the 38 067 (about 19.6%) who wrote mathematical literacy could manage a 40% pass and higher in this sprawling province, where only 65 359 learners reached Grade 12 to write the final examination.

Now, imagine thousands of six-year-olds showing up on the first day of school in a province such as this, excited and energetic because of this brand new experience. Day after day, they find teachers on a go-slow with little interest in them. Many are left alone in classrooms. This goes on for weeks, and slowly but surely that child makes two calculations: they don't care about me, and this is not a great way to spend my time. Before long, that once-upbeat child has learnt a devastating lesson: you might as well stay at home, come late, leave early or just drop out. After all, who cares?

If this so-called go-slow happened in a factory that made canned fruit, the only loss to the company would be a fall in the production of stuffed cans for sale to the outside world. When the canned fruit are children and the workers are teachers, the damage is incalculable, and over 12 years you get the results of the most ineffective education department in South Africa.

I blame the adults for messing up the futures of our most vulnerable children while they fight their never-ending battles. I blame the parents for not taking to the streets and saying: 'Hell, no, you will not destroy the only ticket the family has for escaping poverty – a good education.'

I blame the politicians for not stamping their authority on this chaotic situation and demanding a return to teaching, rather than watching their backs and their pockets in the year of an elective conference. I blame all of us, myself included, for watching this slow-moving train crash, and not speaking out against the rot.

Black belt in pandering

More policing won't solve the problems

20 December 2012

It was not in the prepared speech. It could not be, for that utterance would surely not pass the editorial vetting of the tripartite alliance readers for whom the mere mention of the word 'inspector' induces uncontrollable political spasms.

So what were those presumably off-the-cuff remarks made by the president in his political report at the opening of the 53rd national elective conference of the ANC?

'I want to see [school] inspectors back. Some might oppose this. Some of our friends in labour even don't like this idea. If they don't, then we will just send them to find teachers not doing their work.'

I have to say, I like the personal stamp of authority: 'I want to see.' They call that leadership. I like the identification of the problem: 'Our friends in labour.' Also, I am sure those 'friends' will not enjoy the irony of being sent on search missions to expose lazy teachers.

I do not for one moment believe that school inspectors will be reintroduced. This is, after all, a political speech. The audience for the inspectors quip was outside the big tent. That audience is the concerned elite – business people and middle-class citizens who, rightly, see a massive social and economic disaster coming down the road if we do not turn the schools around.

But simply sending inspectors into schools would be akin to sending more police to Marikana. The crisis is much more complex than policing the problem into some degree of order.

People, however, say strange things on a political platform. The most bizarre was the ANC's priest, who could hardly contain his partisanship as he blurted out: 'Viva God!' at the end of a solemn prayer. Anyone who has even elementary knowledge of the scriptures from any major religion would know this is blasphemous. How can you wish long life to the Giver of Life? Or should we believe that, at that moment, God was decked in green, yellow and gold, pumping the air as the top six slithered onto the conference stage?

The priest knows, of course, that the audience for that prayer is inside the big tent – his preaching about a 'revolutionary morality' might have had the rest of us rolling on the floor in mirth but, remember, we are outside the tent.

Outside the tent, Mangaung and the streets around campus were littered with dirt as comrades disposed of their rubbish in public spaces. Some travellers slept on pavements and in cars; others washed and shaved on the open road.

The conference opened more than three hours late and those outside the tent drew the logical conclusion that, if you cannot open on time for a conference that was planned a year in advance, why should we expect textbooks to be delivered on time?

Inside the tent, the microphones did not work and the lack of air-conditioning during a Free State summer was bound to seduce comrades into a state of slumber, which was happily caught on cameras belonging to those outside the tent.

Outside the tent, the media insisted there was a bloody contest coming – Afrikaans papers even referred to a *slagorder* (slaughtering order) in reference to rival slates. Inside the tent, there was calm because comrades knew that the Jacob Zuma slate would win. Nobody inside the tent questioned why the suspects of a bomb plot were conveniently arrested in the opening days of the conference, generating huge sympathy among the followers of the ruling party. Only days later would it be claimed there was no link between the said would-be bombers and the tent.

There were two moral revolutionaries at the conference.

Outside the tent was journalist Gaye Davis, who resigned from her job after her newspaper's editor refused to pull a story announcing that Cyril Ramaphosa had declined nomination for the position of deputy president of the party.

Listen to this: 'Ethically I cannot [publicly] distance myself from the story while remaining in the employ of Independent Newspapers,' she said.

Inside the tent, Kgalema Motlanthe must have known he would be defeated in the vote for the party presidency. But he understands democracy and that it is important to model democratic practice by allowing the branches that nominated him to express their wishes at the conference.

Viva the real revolutionary morality, viva!

'Clever' slur lives on

Seventy-six years on and we still despise clever black people

22 November 2012

The year is 2012, the accuser a black president. Our leader says some blacks 'become too clever' and 'become the most eloquent in criticising themselves about their own traditions and everything'. Further, if this continues, 'whose traditions will [their children] practise?'

The year is 1936, the accuser the Committee on Native Education, pronouncing thus on black people: 'There is still strong opposition to their education because it makes him "cheeky" [and] it makes him turn against his culture and his people.'

The charge is the same – education makes 'clever blacks' who must be restrained; they must be locked into their 'own' cultures, for too much education makes them misfits within society.

Seventy-six years apart and we still despise clever blacks.

I have heard endless repetition of the sentence: 'He's black, but very smart.' You will, of course, never hear this qualifying 'but' in reference to the intelligence of the pigmentally challenged. So what is going on here?

As more than one commentator has correctly observed, this presidential comment must be read with other statements from on high casting aspersions on book knowledge and mere education.

Any sign of a clever black – like an accent that is not 'traditional' or musical choices that are not 'black' – invites ridicule and resentment. Blacks are cast in a mould that is firm and fixed, unaffected by a changing world.

Instead of placing a high premium on the intellect we, in fact, attack those who think for themselves.

More than one political party insists on shutting down independent opinion even in the face of undemocratic practices and offensive utterances – even calling for a law to punish critics of the powerful.

We are slowly becoming a society that has effectively whipped critics into submission; to think for yourself is to raise querying eyebrows about who you really are. To speak fluently and perceptively is to raise concerns about cultural drift.

The people occupying centre stage in the ferment sweeping the country have become the new norm. So what if the semi-literate miners first killed security guards? Or what if poorly educated farmworkers set fire to vineyards? Or what if the unskilled truckers stoned and wounded hard-working truck drivers on major roads?

Let's focus rather on their plight as underpaid, exploited workers, not on wanton destruction of property. We valorise violent, uncouth, dangerous behaviour. We make victims (again) out of the poor.

Not a single analyst has asked the question: Why did we have to wait for the violence before we took the plight of exploited workers seriously? And nobody asked how the situation could have been different if we had functional schools for all learners and effective, credible post-school training programmes for those who left school early.

'What do we fight about between development plans?' I asked government officials this week.

While powerful economies in Asia set uncompromising standards for education, we destroy the already slim opportunities and vulnerable institutions we need to build strong and durable social systems. While modern education systems recognise the transforming power of 21st-century technologies to create new social, cultural and economic relations across borders, our leaders *klap* clever blacks and remind them to stay in their predestined cultural enclaves.

While more and more young people are transforming their own identities through social and technological relations that break down primordial attachments, we still snigger at black people who achieve in science and the humanities because they no longer talk like 'us' and bow at the altar of ancient traditions.

A clever black just won the American elections. He did this by recognising one simple thing: the world had changed and America had changed. Those old, traditional values built around the often offensive preferences of white men with conservative and traditional values no longer mattered.

Changing demographics and new technologies could be mobilised to create a new kind of society. Instead of dragging people back into an often-romanticised past, the one-time professor held up to young and old a vision of a more hopeful future in which green technologies and digital education would alter lives.

To have won so emphatically in the midst of an economic recession, this black man must have been clever indeed.

How to heal the nation in seven simple steps[*]

We need seven human qualities to transform the healing professions

6 September 2012

I wish to speak to you this morning about the seven human qualities required for transformation of the helping professions. By the helping professions I mean those occupations which have as their primary orientation the duty to serve others. I am thinking of social work, teaching, doctoring and, in your case, nursing.

You do well, as nursing educators, in training young people for basic competence in your profession. But what about those soft skills, which are actually hard skills, required to turn young nurses into more than well-oiled machines and make them well-rounded professionals? I can hear you saying of your charges: I can train you how to set up a drip, but how do I train you not to be one?

In a country as broken and angry as ours, I cannot think of a more important duty than to prepare nursing professionals to heal not only physical wounds but our invisible wounds as we emerge from a bitter past and a still-bitter present.

[*] This is a transcription of the Keynote Address to the Nursing Education Association in East London on 4 September 2012.

I wish to suggest that there are seven human qualities of critical importance in the preparation of nurses as well as other professionals.

1. The capacity to care (working for others)

A group of clinical heads of a well-known hospital was complaining to me about 'the lack of' (a common South African way to start a conversation) things they needed. One of them told me about children who have to wait for hours for urgent paediatric care. 'Would that child have to wait if it was your own flesh and blood?' I asked. 'No,' said the head, 'I would rush to provide immediate care no matter what.'

2. The capacity for diligence (working hard)

What destroys this country is a culture of laziness. We work only to the clock. Managers fear public holidays on a Thursday for our so-called workers will agitate for a long weekend. Any minute over normal time and we demand more money. Ironically, this culture of laziness is especially evident in the public professions.

3. The capacity for efficiency (working fast)

We are slow. Watch a typical nurse or teacher walk in the workplace. They are slow, often overweight, and move without a care in the world. With coffee mugs in hand and casual conversations about the night before, there is a characteristic slowness as if the patients in the bed or the pupils in the classroom did not matter at all.

4. The capacity for joy (working inwards)

Ever noticed a happy nurse skipping down the aisle between beds as if (s)he was filled with the joy of service? I do not meet people like that in the professions any more. Their body language signals depression, and communicates without fail the message that work is a burden and that the professional showing up is in fact a favour to the patient.

5. The capacity for organisation (working smart)

When I see a disorganised office I assume a disorganised mind; someone without the capacity to plan, and to organise in advance. This is a crucial skill, for it is impossible to deliver a service well without knowing the basics of organising and distributing limited resources for the benefit of others.

6. The capacity for anticipation (working ahead)

One of the qualities of a professional is the ability to use knowledge to anticipate the future and plan for a crisis. Yet this simple competence is often lacking in professionals because too often we function as simple workers on the receiving end of decisions rather than as active and autonomous decision-makers ourselves.

7. The capacity for change (working to make a difference)

All professions face this challenge: how do you prevent young people from losing their drive and idealism once they begin work? This is difficult, but we cannot produce new teachers or social workers or nurses who behave as if they are victims of their circumstances.

So how do we train for these qualities in young professionals, such as nurses? You can do it through the example you set as nursing educators; through the love that is conveyed in modelling an ethic of care; through the discipline that is imposed on errant behaviour; through the selectivity that is applied in the choice of those entering the profession; through the practice time that is afforded, under supervision, before entering the profession; and through the values that are extolled and upheld daily in the course of preparing young nurses for the workplace.

2030 vision is blind

How do you enact lofty ideals in a society trapped in despair?

23 August 2012

I felt for Trevor Manuel last Thursday. In the same week that he handed over the revised National Development Plan: Vision for 2030 to the president in Cape Town, at the other end of the country a bloody massacre left bodies sprawled across a dusty stretch of veld in the North West mining settlement of Marikana.

It was a horrific reminder of one of the most difficult challenges facing the development plan – enacting lofty ideals into a society trapped in despair.

There is nothing wrong with the plan in theory; but in practice there is everything wrong with its overly optimistic assumption that we can easily become the society it envisions.

The past few months have been very difficult, as I again worked my way through rural South Africa.

In hospitals, I was alarmed by the tangible fear of safety for health workers and patients (imagine a patient being raped in her bed); the constant complaints of a lack of equipment and basic medicines; and the perennial shortage of staff.

I watched in horror as old people waited for hours for our politicians to arrive; no sense of urgency or respect. I witnessed again how pensioners wait in queues for days on end in a rural village. I talked in a classroom, and the teacher never showed up at all.

Manuel is right about one thing: this is not a money problem.

It is a problem of a broken society that simply does not take people seriously.

It would be very dangerous at this point to valorise the miners (ten people died at the hands of miners before the televised massacre), and especially their rival bosses, who in fighting and insulting each other on a Sunday television programme demonstrated how the Marikana massacre happened in the first place.

There is a spectacular lack of leadership, and the mining company appears to be a big part of the problem.

In other words, the kind of society and the kind of leadership we have must dramatically change its value system and its human commitments if the National Development Plan is to even stand a chance of implementation.

Let's take the plan's proposed measures for education: 'Increase the quality of education so that all children have at least two years of preschool education and all children in Grade 3 can read and write.'

You have to have a heart of stone not to agree with this goal.

But how is this going to happen in a society that can't take care of the 12 million children within the existing school system?

How many ambitious politicians, dead and alive, have sworn that our children will become literate and numerate by a certain grade or date?

This is another such promise.

However, in a society which can't get textbooks to schools on time, or install teachers in schools on the first day of the school year, or prevent unions from destabilising the poorest of schools month-in and year-out, how exactly is this going to be achieved?

In a society where every education tender above R1 million is almost guaranteed to draw the attention of corrupt, incompetent and well-connected scoundrels, how is quality pre-school education even possible?

We seem to forget that from the first day of the national school nutrition programme of the 1990s for younger children, there were people robbing this fund.

To achieve the noble goals of the National Development Plan, the authors need to drastically recalibrate and ask whether we have the kind of society in which such goals are possible. It is not enough to say we must all pull together in the same direction.

It is not enough to set noble goals for 2030 when many of those cheering the plan will be dead or retired. It is not enough to appeal to our values when the brutal reality is that we all do not share the same core values on, for example, the welfare of young children.

If Marikana teaches us anything it is this: our society is not ready for this kind of National Development Plan.

Fiddling the books

Why can we deliver beer but not textbooks?

2 August 2012

'There are 26 000 shebeens in South Africa,' mused a friend the other day, 'and every week a major breweries company successfully delivers crates of liquor to every one of them.'

He continues: 'There are also 26 000 schools in this country, and yet we cannot deliver textbooks to all of them. We do not have a skills crisis.'

I laughed, and then I cried, for in this seemingly absurd comparison there was more than a grape of truth. So what explains this reality that we can deliver beer to shebeens but not textbooks to schools?

To state the obvious, the company makes money out of the delivery of beer. If it does not deliver, it does not get money. Imagine if this principle were applied in education. The textbook delivery company does not get a cent unless it can prove that it successfully delivered the right textbooks in the right amounts to the right schools at the right time – namely, before the school year even starts. The problem will go away.

You are not even asking the liquor company to care deeply about the client, though it would be nice if textbook companies were motivated to promote learning among the youth. You deliver a service to the standards set by the client, and you get your money. Imagine if teachers were paid in relation to the results of their pupils. Your pupils can read and write? Collect your payment at the end of the month.

Of course this is not going to happen because South Africans have refined the art of deflecting blame to someone else, even if that person has been dead for 40 years, as is the case with HF Verwoerd.

But there is something else that would happen if the breweries in question did not deliver the beer; the client would go elsewhere with their money – to the competition.

Imagine the schools were given their allocation of textbook monies directly, and they could purchase textbooks from the local supplier themselves.

Or, the textbook companies would have to come to the school and make the case to supply the textbooks directly to the client. Once again, the problem could potentially be solved.

This also will not happen because textbooks represent the new site of struggle, if you forgive a perverse application of a once-progressive language.

If schools could purchase their own textbooks, you would destroy a corrupt class of budding millionaires waiting in the supply chain line to rip off the state and enrich themselves.

Here is a bitter irony: some of the same comrades who worked in the department of education in the early years of democracy then lambasted publishers for making money from textbooks, and tried to sell the crooked idea that under Outcomes-Based Education, schools did not need textbooks since learning materials should be developed from the contexts of learning.

Those former comrades are now the multimillionaire owners and CEOs of quasi-private textbook companies infuriated by recent exposés of alleged incompetence and corruption in the delivery of these learning materials. The chickens have come home to roost.

The problem precedes the 1990s. It is common knowledge that many white bureaucrats in the former race-based education system would write school textbooks themselves and deliver them to publishing houses, to then retire as millionaires. By then restricting 'the list' of official texts from which a school could order their prescribed books, the corrupt bureaucrat could ensure an instant 'bestseller'.

One university gained notoriety by condoning the practice of professors writing the textbooks to support study guides for their own courses.

Unsuspecting students had to buy these expensive books from the publishers, and so made their professors rich.

In a further act of greed, the professors would slightly revise the textbooks every year in a fresh edition so that new students could not purchase the previous years' textbooks at a reduced price.

Of course, there is nothing wrong with professors writing textbooks to be used in their classes; but when that practice is unregulated by the employer, and when what is at stake is not 15 students in a philosophy class but

30 000 students in a sociology class, then the table is laid for massive corruption.

Rather than commissioning four or five hasty reports in a clumsy attempt to put out the flames that resulted from the textbook scandal in Limpopo province, government should rather commission a more comprehensive study of the textbook industry.

The nexus of textbooks and money should be thoroughly investigated for corruption.

The use of independent, private companies with a track record of success should be non-negotiable.

The involvement of former government employees or political operatives in this industry must be stopped.

Placing the power for purchasing textbooks in the hands of the schools should be considered. Imposing a strong system of accountability on textbook providers is essential – your contract should contain a specific clause that you do not get paid, or you risk a massive financial penalty for non-delivery or partial delivery of textbooks.

Of course, ministers of state should be held accountable, and resigning is the honourable thing to do. But it will not solve the much deeper problem of deeply vested interests in the textbook industry in which, I am dead certain, some very powerful people in this country have a silent stake.

Another day of pain

Young men on the Cape Flats have a better chance of getting into Pollsmoor Prison than UCT

26 July 2012

'Two to three dead bodies a day,' says my friend as we talk about the ongoing gang warfare he bears witness to in a part of the Cape Flats.

'Two to three bodies a day,' he repeats, as if I did not hear the first time.

It has been a while since I have seen so much misery in one day.

My day starts in a windswept area called Delft. As my car enters the gate at 8.50 am, some children are already leaving the school, slowly drifting nowhere.

'Please go for a walk,' the principal says as I enter the school hall. He needs time to calm the children before I can even speak to them.

This is rough territory. Many of the children come from Blikkiesdorp.

'The name says it all,' offers one of the deputies, referring to tin shacks down the road.

In one classroom a group of boys are eating samp and beans from a cold plate as if they have not seen food for a long time.

These young men at Hindle High School stand a much greater chance of getting into Pollsmoor Prison than the University of Cape Town (UCT) – and they know it.

To the other side of the Cape Flats is Lavender Hill High School, a five-minute drive from where I grew up in Retreat.

As I look down at the hundreds of young people in front of me, I wonder what I could possibly say that might change the chances of these beautiful minds. The pupils here know other children who have fallen to 'stray bullets'.

Later, while driving out of the school gates, I find a small group of very young gangsters waiting to connect with the pupils when they leave the premises.

Why, I don't know. To rob, recruit, intimidate, or to scare?

A lot of children – and mothers – have been buried in these areas recently.

The politician in charge of safety and security (really) speaks first, telling stories about children he has met on the Flats, including one who had six bullets in a tender body. My friends in the area share terrifying stories about funerals.

Anywhere else, where people have money, such a high body count would have led to the place being declared an emergency area while police cars and armed private patrols with huge, new trucks on shiny, high wheels would have been visible everywhere. Not in Lavender Hill or Delft.

There is no question that the army has to be called in simply to stop the haemorrhaging, but then we need to work on long-term solutions.

It is equally clear the state will have to pour massive resources into places like Hanover Park, Langa and Manenberg to create a future for young people.

This problem is not going to go away with piecemeal solutions.

We must provide effective training and productive work for the out-of-school youth to give them a sense of hope beyond the drab, colourless flats of these areas.

We need to declare a real war on drugs so the comfortably established networks of criminals that sustain these endless cycles of chemical dependency are broken.

We should insist on viable community centres with education-rich programmes and activities.

In the long run, there is no other lasting solution than to keep young boys, especially, in school.

But it does not help to send children to school when teachers are not always there and timetables are seldom respected.

With fathers often in prison, with young mothers in cycles of pregnancy, and older mothers often at their wits' end about how to protect their children, the hard reality is that school might be one of the only places left (apart from the churches and mosques) where young people could still be persuaded to change their course.

What warmed my heart at both Hindle and Lavender was the energetic presence of older women who invest their time, skills and resources in these young people by organising choirs, field trips, workshops and motivational speakers.

They do not ask for or receive a cent in return.

Once again, ordinary citizens are holding communities together while the political parties play their sordid games about whether or not to bring in the army.

In the meantime, the children continue to die.

An ugly side to Ugie

Hold onto the good truths in the wake of violence

14 June 2012

Dear Jacky, I cannot think of a worse way in which to start a Monday morning. Your Facebook posting saddened me more than anything I have ever experienced. I am so very sorry.

You wrote:

Good morning, Mr Jansen. WE NEED TO TALK. Our small northeastern Cape community is in deep shock after our headmaster and his wife were brutally attacked in the early hours of Sunday morning.

Linie Gouws died from her injuries and Chris Gouws, principal of Ugie High School, survived the attack. School starts in about an hour. The students are writing exams.

It is going to be such a hard day on everyone, the students who see Chris as a father figure, the teachers, the parents, the community on 'both sides of the Wildebeest River'. The Gouwses have been an integral part of the community for more than 25 years... Do you possibly have any advice for a place which is going through such trauma?

Regards,

Jacky Lamer

(English teacher, Ugie High School)

Shortly after reading your posting, a friend of the family posted on Facebook her own angry record of events.

She wrote (edited):

So, a couple I know was attacked in their rural home this weekend. Managed to make a call to the local police station in between all the stabbing and torture and stuff... No answer. Later, with blood all over and punctured by multiple stab wounds, they manage to drive to the police station and find the cops warming themselves around a cosy little fire and a no-cars-no-can-do response.

I hate general middle-class whining about crime and really take people to task for it, but if we can't trust the police anymore to do the most basic part of their job, then we have to accept that the thin blue line is non-existent (by the way, the woman then died in the car).

I must confess, Jacky, that I probably can say very little, given the terrible pain and anguish you, the pupils and other teachers must be experiencing. But let me try.

First, you have the right to be angry – at the murderers, at the police, at the system, at all of us who failed to protect these precious souls.

You are right to question why it is that two passionate South Africans, who gave their lives to the education of our people, could be the victims of such brutal violence.

And you are right to be concerned about the effects of this senseless eradication of human lives on the impressionable minds of the children in your school and on the motivation of the teachers who, I am sure, already fight incredible odds to give the young people of this rural town a decent chance in life.

But I also need to tell you this: you are not alone.

After I posted your story, hundreds of South Africans from all walks of life contacted me to wish you well, to pray for you, and to stand with you in this hour of need.

You will read many of these messages on my Facebook site.

Please tell the teachers, tell the pupils and tell the community that there are millions of South Africans joining hands with the school and the people of Ugie at this time. You are not alone.

I ask you to keep perspective. In this country of more than 40 million people, there are many more good people than there are bad people.

Above the familiar noise and the wanton violence, hold on to this simple truth. Hard as this might sound, we dare not give up. Too many have died in the struggle for justice and the pursuit of peace in South Africa.

We must, especially at this time, stand firm and stand together, determined that a few wicked people must not destroy the promise of our democracy.

We will join you shortly with counselling and support services and whatever else you might need.

In the meantime, I thought that this note (edited) from one of our students, after reading my Facebook posting, will encourage you and the community at this time:

Mr Gouws was my school principal for a good ten years.

His late wife was our adoptive mother. My heart is weary. I can only imagine the sombre atmosphere at the school. Both were active community leaders.

It is a sad day for the Ugie community. Thanks to him I have now just completed my degree at the University of the Free State.

Chuma Xundu

The middle cannot hold

A collapse of educational authority

10 May 2012

The hand of the director of education in the Western Cape was shaking noticeably as he stretched out his arm to greet me. This was a good man. I knew him from my teenage years as one of those upright young men who just had this way of restoring your faith in humanity. He had devoted his life to education.

He had worked as a senior education official on the violent Flats, where bullets regularly flew across playgrounds and where young men had long dropped out of cold-hearted schools to find succour and security in a local gang.

He had matured in leadership to lead scores of officials in building effective schools in difficult areas.

The shaking hand of my long-time friend put a lump in my throat. This was a humble man with a heart for education who worked 18 hours a day against great odds to keep our schools together.

Most of the people I meet in his position across the country are not like him. They are officious, arrogant and often lack the competence required for directoral leadership in education. Many are party hacks, people who regard themselves as deployees of their political masters.

Yet here was a good man whose body bore the scars of running schools in the townships. I dared not ask him about the shaking hand; I respect him too much.

He volunteered this story.

Not too long ago he had made the decision, with the approval of his seniors in politics, to close down a highly ineffective township school that was wasting the time and money of the youth from the area; it was not even an officially recognised school.

When the decision was made, pupils of the school took him hostage and blockaded the offices for hours.

'Jonathan, they humiliated me over and over again.'

He should not have told me that; I could feel the pain of his words and the anxiety it produced in my colleague, my friend.

Few people write or think about this special species in education: the hard-working, competent and committed official caught between militant or uninterested teachers and hard-headed politicians. These directors and their deputies are placed under enormous pressure by their seniors to deliver on impossible mandates in hostile school environments.

They are ignored by some schools, ridiculed by others, and the weaker among them are co-opted into the political manoeuvres of the dominant unions. They are never recognised when schools do well, but are castigated when schools fare poorly.

It is the good ones I'm talking about.

When pupils also turn on these bureaucrats sandwiched between teachers, unions and politicians, their limited authority is stripped bare.

At the root of the crisis facing the committed, even idealistic professional in education is this collapse of authority.

They are called inspectors by the militant teachers who refuse to accept that the supervision of education and educators is fundamental to building and sustaining good schools in any democracy. In several provinces, these supervisors of education are regularly refused access to delinquent schools for a simple reason: they will witness the rot children have to put up with because of failing teachers and principals.

A good principal, in turn, will face daily pressure from the militants if he insists on simple things like teachers showing up on time. A good teacher dares not be over-enthusiastic about sticking to timetables and assigning regular homework, for it shows up the lazy bastards sunning themselves in the staffroom during regular periods.

The politician, on the other hand, wants results, not because he or she cares that much about children, but because they sign KPAs (Key Performance Area agreements) with their political seniors to improve results by any means possible.

So the sandwiched officials now have to put pressure on schools to perform – on schools that are not enthusiastic about their presence in the first place – or face the wrath of seniors in air-conditioned buildings far from the arrhythmia of township schools.

Many of these officials simply give up, content to play the much safer role of messenger boys and girls carrying official information between the district or circuit office and the school. Others leave the profession for fear of ending up where many of their colleagues do: in a doctor's office being treated for chronic stress, with shaking hands.

WE NEED TO ACT IN HOPE

'The critical ingredient is courage.'

Simple refusal to hate

Inspiration from the Middle East

27 October 2011

For a Palestinian man whose daughters were maimed and killed – one decapitated by a shell from an Israeli tank – Izzeldin Abuelaish is astonishingly without any bitterness.

In response to this unspeakable family tragedy, the Gaza doctor established a foundation called Daughters for Life, which provides scholarships for studies to girls from the Middle East, including Jewish girls from inside Israel.

I could see quiet tears in the mesmerised campus audience in the face of such uncommon grace.

The famous physician, an expert in infertility, has delivered babies on both sides of the contested borders of the old country. When once asked whether he hated Jews, he asked: 'Which Jews should I hate? Those who are my friends or whose babies I delivered?'

When his surviving eldest daughter was asked by CNN, 'Doesn't this [the death of her twin sister at the hands of the Israeli military] make you angry?' her unearthly response was: 'Angry with whom?'

You are mistaken if you think that the Abuelaish family's commitment to reconciliation is an alternative to social justice; their stance makes social justice possible.

He uses his position as an eminent physician to press the Israeli authorities to change their oppressive policies.

He presents a powerful case within the US to press the main supporters of the Israeli government for justice towards the Palestinians. He speaks openly, everywhere, about oppression and injustice against his countrymen and women – and he is heard precisely because he does this from the rare platform of inclusion and embrace.

I am astounded by the ways in which this humble man embraces his many identities – from his roots in a Palestinian refugee camp; his religious devotions as a Muslim; his academic ambitions as a professor in Toronto; and his commitments as the father of surviving children whose mother died of leukaemia just before the Israeli shell landed in his daughters' bedroom.

His perspective is informed by his discipline. So he argues that trying to resolve the historic conflicts between Israelis and Palestinians can be done only by recognising the vulnerabilities of both sides.

'It's like conjoined twins; trying to separate and save one could kill the other,' he says.

'And how does one prevent children from inheriting bitterness and hatred? It's like diabetes; prevention is better than cure; get to the problem early.'

Are current strategies working to resolve the conflict?

'No, because as doctors you learn not to treat the symptoms of the problem but the underlying causes; the causes include the occupation and the loss of Palestinian land; that is what must be dealt with.'

Once you start reading his book, *I Shall Not Hate*, it grabs you as you find yourself recalling the startling similarities of the Palestinian struggle to the struggle against apartheid. His stories of the daily humiliation of Palestinians crossing checkpoints to work on the other side of these inhumane borders reminds you of the pettiness of racial discrimination that slowly builds up the anger of a *gatvol* people.

But Abuelaish does not tell these stories to inflame, the way we do as if to justify our anger and resentment. He shares these stories to remind us of the urgency of resolving one of the longest human conflicts in history.

Most of all, he tells these stories of oppression alongside stories of hope. After the signing of the Oslo Accord – and the withdrawal of Israeli tanks – the children threw not stones but candles and flowers.

In a week in which we called Indians 'coolies' and in which judges pushed for a place on the KwaZulu-Natal bench by pitting our ethnic African identity against that of our Indian brothers, the Gaza doctor taught us how to remember and how to account for our past and our future. His pedagogy is faultless – tell the stories of tragedy in concert with the stories of triumph.

I stare at the well-set, talkative man in amazement. A million questions run through my head, like: 'What is the source of your compassion and your ability to forgive, when your flesh and blood lies submerged under the rubble of a collapsed bedroom?'

And then you realise the ordinary man sitting in front of you was recently nominated for the Nobel Peace Prize, and that he might very well be the Nelson Mandela of the Middle East who brings together Israeli Jews and Palestinian Arabs in an unlikely settlement.

Courage to change

How do we behave in different social spaces in South Africa?

20 October 2011

What got me onto this line of thinking was a fascinating pair of books that I just finished reading, one by social psychologist Claude Steele titled *Whistling Vivaldi*. He retells a story of the discomforts of a black man when he walked through a white American neighbourhood and observed the racial fears of white pedestrians: body language stiffened; couples walked more closely together; and eye contact was studiously avoided. Then he noticed that, when he whistled melodies from Vivaldi, the white folk relaxed and became more comfortable with the passing presence of the black man. Fascinating. Steele's book is about what he calls stereotype threats and how to overcome them.

The other intriguing book on this theme is by Yale sociologist Elijah Anderson titled *The Cosmopolitan Canopy* in which the author reports on a study of social spaces and how white and black Americans encounter each other in the middle-class shopping malls compared with streets through rough neighbourhoods, compared with downmarket shopping centres.

There is a lot of civility to go around in the middle-class spaces; here people are comfortable with each other, and the social rules allow for greeting and even the exchange of light banter between strangers. But change the setting, and the relationships stiffen.

There is a lot of this going on in South Africa as well. A white group walking through Soweto in the dead of night would be scared witless. But call the occasion the Fifa Soccer World Cup or the Super 15 rugby finals, and the rules of encounter change so that small and large groups of whites venture easily into black homes on weekends.

Over the years I have observed such unconscious space management among white and black students at several South African universities. Without any seating arrangements being made, black students who are strangers to one another gravitate towards racial blocks in the university classroom, and the same for white students. When you point this out to either side, they first express surprise that this is noticed, and then come the defensive parries: 'We feel more comfortable with people from our own cultures or who speak our own languages.'

Of course the students in these uniracial groups are themselves often from very different cultures, but in this country 'culture' has become the more comfortable substitute in our language for 'skin'.

We all understand how racial mastery, myth and memories implanted in our minds over centuries continue to afflict us even when the legal barriers to normal human interaction have been broken down. We are not reacting to the present; we are carrying the burden of history. We are not bad people. We simply do not know how to overcome the present past. But there is hope.

'Would you join me for worship at the Abyssinian Baptist Church in Harlem tomorrow?' asks a friend.

I sat to consider this otherwise-normal request from a fellow South African. I smiled, hopeful of our future, for the person asking me to go to church is a devout Muslim. The space he planned to enter was evangelical Christian, a familiar setting – theologically if not culturally – from my childhood upbringing in the Cape. The idea of being invited to church by a Muslim was a special South African moment.

How did my Muslim friend overcome centuries of racial and religious brainwashing? It starts by recognising our interconnectedness. Our identities are not unchanging racial essences inscribed by the divine. This was the ultimate lie of apartheid's ideologues. We come from each other's bosoms. We are shaped and defined by each other. That is why we miss each other, and miss home, when we leave this country. I have witnessed how hard we try to connect in Afrikaans or isiZulu in faraway lands, just to remind ourselves of our common heritage.

Our transformation continues when we realise that by breaking through our ethnic and faith entrapments we are not 'giving up' anything. My friend is not less Muslim because of his openness to Baptist worship in Harlem.

The critical ingredient is courage. Our tribal or herd instincts in this country are still very strong. We look around, so to speak, before we step across those invisible lines that still separate us by race, ethnicity, and religion. The more adults who cross those lines without fearing the charge of 'kaffirboetie' or 'coconut' by the tribalists around us, the easier it will be for our children to be human.

A day in SA's miracle school

An infectious learning culture

8 September 2011

It is 4 pm on 6 September 2011. Every child is in school; not a soul has left.

Every teacher is on site, not a car has moved. I follow the pairs of neat, black shoes gathered in two rows down the length of the inner courtyard of the school – there is no school hall, and there is no loudhailer. My voice would have to carry through the open air.

Every shoe is brightly polished. Every window is whole. Every blade of grass seems perfectly cut. Every child's head is smoothly shaven. Every pupil is clothed in a spotless grey uniform.

The short principal lifts his arm high and with the thumbs-up signal, more than 1 000 high school students fall quiet, instantly. I am, once again, inside South Africa's best high school. It is where I come again and again when I despair about the future of our country. This is my holy place of annual pilgrimage: Zwelibanzi High School; Umlazi, J-section, Durban; principal: Sibusiso Maseko.

It has been a tiring day that will end at the grounds of Hilton College with talks to boys and teachers on what are easily the most beautiful school grounds anywhere in South Africa.

But the day started early in a place called Wentworth, where four schools gathered their pupils for me to address what the invitation described as a cancer eroding the spirit of the youth and community – drugs and gangs.

It does not take long to get the children hyped up about their futures in a dismal, colourless community where fathers are seldom present and girls fall pregnant too early. The only recognition boys can achieve is in the comfort – and safety – of a local gang. But here in Wentworth a combination of courageous teachers and resilient community leaders are fighting back against formidable odds.

Then on to a school with impressive resources and one of the most inspiring principals I've ever met. It is St Mary's DSG in Kloof, and I am astounded by the values-based education that the young girls learn and how attuned they are, black and white, to the responsibility that comes with privilege.

But it is at Zwelibanzi, with its rudimentary classrooms and its elementary facilities, that South Africa's future will be decided. The computer laboratory has very few machines; but two boys are working during the lunch break on finding treatments for ischemic stroke patients from electronic resources.

'What makes your school different from other schools in the area?' I ask one girl who is mopping the floors of her classroom.

Her answer comes straight from the psychology textbooks on motivation: 'Our teachers expect much from us.'

Both pianos are hopelessly out of tune. But the children learn 'voice' and the music teacher has collected basic resources to teach the children to sing.

'So what do you want to become one day?' I ask another group.

They fight for the visitor's attention as planned careers range from pilots to lawyers to chartered accountants.

'Why not teaching?' I ask instinctively.

'Too much stress,' they answer, almost in unison.

It is a chilling reminder that what enables a school like this to defy the odds means having a principal and teachers who absorb enormous stress to give these children a chance at success. Then comes the more astounding announcement. The school only closes at 4 pm for the lower grades. Grade 12 pupils continue at the grey-uniformed school till eight that night. I have to sit to catch my breath.

There must be all kinds of psychological and physiological reasons why keeping children this late might not be the best idea.

'What about travelling home that late at night?' we ask the principal.

'The parents arrange taxis,' he answers.

The community stands rock-solid behind the school's ambitions.

The bell rings, but there is no rush to the gate for the pre-Grade 12 pupils. They love being here. The Grade 12s head back to class; and then a scene I will never forget. Coming into the school gates at this late hour of the day are children with red uniforms, others with blue uniforms, and more. These are Grade 12s from other high schools who want to join the teach-and-learn-until-8 pm group. It is infectious, this powerful learning culture at Zwelibanzi.

I no longer worry about the thugs circling Luthuli House. Their replacement leaders will come from this sacred place inside Umlazi.

Saluting science teacher Saleh

The greatest science teacher I have ever known

18 August 2011

'My boy, if your marks do not improve I will dissolve you in sulphuric acid!'

The voice in the science laboratory next to my biology class was that of the inimitable Saleh Adams. Every student who knew the man understood this great humanist lacked the capacity to hurt the proverbial fly, but right there and then the student being threatened with a corrosive chemical must have felt as if some great impending doom was upon him.

My class roared with laughter as the meaningless threat travelled through the thin walls separating our classrooms. I subdued my own laughter, careful to show respect for a colleague in the face of students, the way teachers those days used to do.

This week Adams, the greatest physical science teacher I have ever known, passed away in his home in the scenic Bo Kaap area of Cape Town.

Those were dark days teaching in the ruins of District Six. Most of our students' homes had been destroyed by the bulldozers of the apartheid regime. More and more children were coming from the faraway areas of the Cape Flats by train as if in defiance of their forced dislocation. Those heartless ideologues of apartheid had actually built police barracks on the grounds where historic homes of black people once stood. Thoughtless whites moved into the area as if this was the most normal thing to do. Many of our students struggled, and they had every reason to act out their anger at what we called 'the system' inside the school and its impoverished classrooms.

But you were playing with your life if you thought that you could enter the physics and chemistry classroom of Mr Adams, as he was called then, and throw a political tantrum. As a young teacher, I often stood outside his classroom and peered inside to see how he managed to not only hold the attention of teenagers around something as dry as the periodic table of elements, but get them to excel in that subject every student feared. His results through the old 'matric' were exceptional for mainly poor students, and the demands for his skilful teaching forced him to teach after-school classes in other parts of Cape Town.

It was, however, his manner that most caught my attention. He was always dressed immaculately, his black-grey hair flattened with precision. In class, the uncreased white lab coat came over the pressed suit during experiments; where he got all those chemicals and glass equipment was a mystery when the typical excuse of the township teacher blamed 'the system' for the lack of resources.

It is hard to explain this, but the teachers of that generation spoke perfect English with the kind of flowing, measured, intellectual tone that demanded the same kind of eloquent expression from the students. The teaching plan was perfectly organised; delivery smoothly done;

homework regularly assigned; feedback faithfully given; and assessment records perfectly stored.

There was something Adams (and his generation) demonstrated in his life as a teacher that I will always remember: to him, teaching and activism were the same thing.

It was by teaching children well that their academic futures looked bright despite 'the system'.

It was by modelling professional behaviour that their respect for teachers and teaching was secured. It was by holding up high moral standards in his life that saw his students try to emulate his personal example.

And so I tried, as a young teacher, to be like Mr Adams – I could never find in it myself to call him by his first name. So I also wore a white coat. I flattened my hair. I tried to teach with flair and passion, like him. From my own pocket I bought and put to sleep rabbits and frogs for dissections. I wanted my 'bio' students to have the same laboratory experience as his 'physics' students. I threatened the innocent youngsters with my chemical of choice, chloroform. But try as I did, I knew, and my students surely knew, I could never rise to the standards of teaching and the example of living that Adams so easily expressed at Trafalgar High School.

Small wonder hundreds of people, many past students among them, flocked to his funeral this week. To some he was Imam Saleh Adams, a devout Muslim; to others he was Dr Saleh Adams, the accomplished scholar of misconceptions in science learning; to all he was Mr Saleh Adams, distinguished physical science teacher.

Unionless and united to learn

Leadership committed to being accountable for learning

11 August 2011

The road trip into rural Umkomaas is deceptively beautiful.

You drive along a winding road surrounded by green hills looking down on the spectacular ocean below. This is the land that Alan Paton wrote about.

On this warm morning in rural KwaZulu-Natal, you remind yourself that the rest of the country is shivering in the bitter cold of a concluding winter.

'Everything keeps going right,' I think as I travel with board members from the Toyota Foundation to visit one of the schools they support.

The dip down one of the many hills brings you alongside the gate of Dlambula Primary, and the first thing you see is a beautiful garden, built by the children. You enter a rock-solid school building, built by the community. You see the elementary science equipment, bought with funds raised from the community. You see children beautifully dressed in their brown uniforms, paid for by the community. The singing that greets the small group of visitors lifts the human spirit as the melodies seem to drift across the hills down to the valley below.

But what grips the visitor is the buzz in the rectangle of classrooms surrounding the sparse inner courtyard.

Every class has a teacher pacing energetically down the narrow aisles between rows of desks. In one classroom the children are reading aloud to two adults. In another they are writing furiously. I can see a vibrant question-and-answer session in a third classroom. From another angle big boys are carrying pots of food, for the lunch break is close. Not a single child drifting aimlessly out of the classroom. Not a single teacher in the staffroom, for there is none.

I move towards the primary school children in the choir to check whether this rare picture of energetic teaching and learning is a set-up. I am going to test their language skills, and so I ask them some tough questions in English, no doubt a second or third or even fourth language for these little ones. They speak better English than some of the university students I once taught from this area; their vocabulary is extensive; their insight and anticipation of the questioning brilliant.

The smallest child recites the most beautiful story in isiZulu, a gift for which she won some prize. I pose the problem $\frac{1}{2} \times \frac{3}{4}$, a problem beyond the grade level of the class I am standing in, and a young girl jumps up with the correct answer.

But it is the confidence of these rural children that surprises me, their capacity to hold down serious conversation with a professor from another place without the slightest hint of discomfort.

Here's the rub. The classrooms are hopelessly overcrowded with more than 60 children in the first class I peer into. There are enough teachers but not enough classrooms, so grades share a class. The solidly cemented classrooms have roofs that leak in the winter. The blackboards are so old that the chalked writing is hardly visible.

It is tough teaching at Dlambula Primary, and even tougher growing up in the community around it. A senior teacher speaks with emotion about a girl in the school whose mother was beaten, robbed and raped, and her body then placed on a nearby railway line. Fortunately, the train driver stopped in time and the body was removed from the coming crush. The girl is still in the school; the body still in the morgue. We all sit with lumps in the throat.

How can a school be so good, so resilient, despite the difficult social and economic conditions of the area? How does a poor community give of its last cents to build this school? How do teachers keep going despite the horrible traumas that children bring into the school from their broken homes? How do the children stand up over and over again, determined not to succumb to the devastation around them?

It's quite simple, really. When you meet the principal, you sense strong leadership. When you listen to his deputy principal and the senior (all women) teachers, you sense a collective commitment to simple things, like 'the children come first'. The school is spotlessly clean; always a sign of a strong learning culture. The chair of the governing body, a simple man, is also impressive, for this is his school and he plays a key role in keeping his leadership accountable for learning.

The parents did not build this school only to sit back and not participate in what happens there.

There was no sign of the teachers' union.

Triumph of the human spirit

Recognising our unsung heroes

23 June 2011

The wrinkled old man addressing the captains of finance and insurance on the shiny upper floors of Alexander Forbes in Sandton was not supposed to be there.

He is the fellow who rises early in the morning to unlock the doors and to switch on the urns and the heaters in order to warm up the buildings for teachers and students at the famed Jeppe High School for Boys in Johannesburg; around midnight he locks up the school again and makes sure everything is in order at an hour when the youngsters and their educators are already tucked away in their warm beds. For some time the old man lived in the attic of the stables near a rugby field on the Jeppe grounds. So why is a school caretaker addressing the serious suits?

'This is only the beginning,' says the old man at the podium with a boldness you dare not question.

'I am now planning for my PhD.'

If you knew the story of the caretaker, you would be a fool to doubt that it was only a matter of time before you would have to call him Dr Martin Ledwaba.

He started as 'the cleaner' at Jeppe in the early 1970s. It is the kind of language that concealed what he really did – serve as 'science laboratory assistant' to the white schoolboys. The fancy title applied only to whites in the employ of the Transvaal Education Department.

But Ledwaba did not only prepare the lab materials for group work or teacher demonstrations. He was actively learning high school science as he went along. He would become the resident expert on every science experiment in the syllabus. Successive generations of boys would later testify that they passed physics and chemistry in part because of the knowledge gained from this unmatriculated cleaner doubling as an unofficial laboratory instructor.

His knowledge of science grew, as did his confidence as a teacher.

Ledwaba then decided to himself study matric biology and physical science by correspondence while doing his day job. But matric part-time was not enough. Ledwaba then pursued a formal teacher's qualification, and recently completed his National Professional Diploma in Education in the natural sciences. He is now a qualified science teacher, but decided this was not enough. The PhD beckons, and he gives the shocked suits at Alexander Forbes a wonderful fright by declaring specific dates for the achievement of the honours, masters and doctorate. Wet lines run down the stern faces in the room.

There is a hidden history in the story of this newly minted teacher.

It is a story about black South Africans who, over the many decades of apartheid, gained great knowledge and competence in specialist fields while doing the menial work to which their race predestined them, in the thinking of their masters. Some were lucky, like Ledwaba, the science teacher. A more well-known case is that of Hamilton Naki, the gardener who turned medical assistant to heart surgeon Christiaan Barnard, and who was reputed to have been exceptional in animal transplants.

Barnard himself once said of Naki that 'given the opportunity, he would have been a better surgeon than me'.

How many thousands more black South Africans – in nursing, medicine, law, teaching, accounting and more – learnt through observation and practice to equal and extend the competence of those privileged to carry title and recognition by virtue of their skin?

We had an interesting idea about how to deal with great learners and achievers like Ledwaba and Naki; it was a policy called 'the recognition of prior learning'. But this policy, instead of being a facilitative mechanism for tens of thousands of bricklayers, mechanics, engineering practitioners and more, became a huge administrative and bureaucratic barrier to those who could not enjoy formal recognition for their skills and experiences. Try it, and you will see how impossible it is for anyone to gain due recognition for prior experience.

My point is this: it is not only about pushing young people through school and university to address the social and economic skills we so urgently need for the 21st century; our task is also to recognise those among us who over decades built competencies across fields, despite the ruthlessness of job reservation and social exclusion, who can also fill the gaps in an underskilled economy.

I can think of no better demonstration of social justice than to give recognition to these incredible South Africans from the generations of our parents and grandparents.

Down's girl makes spirit soar

A speech of unparalleled intelligence, insight and compassion

16 March 2011

I have sat in audiences where I have listened to and interacted with Edward Said, Jürgen Habermas, Oprah Winfrey, Nelson Mandela and a half-dozen Nobel Laureates in the sciences.

But never before have I heard a speech with the intelligence, insight and compassion of a Down's syndrome girl who came to my office three days ago. This is what she said:

As you can see I am a person with Down's Syndrome, which means that I have one extra chromosome in every cell in my body. My grandmother's friends wanted to pray for me to become 'normal' but my mother asked them rather to pray that I would receive the support to reach my full potential as a Down's Syndrome person.

I always knew that I was different. My mother explained to me that the reason why I have more difficulty studying and doing things is because I am a person with Down's Syndrome.

I wondered why people admire Nelson Mandela. When my mother explained that he was in jail for 27 years and stayed positive and loving, I immediately identified with him. Sometimes I feel as if I am in the jail of my own body because

I cannot always say how I feel and many people talk to my mother about me, but not to me, as if I am invisible or cannot speak for myself.

I learn new things every day and sometimes feel sorry for myself because I cannot get married or leave the house in the same way that my sisters do. I know Gustaaf, my Down's friend for the past 12 years, will not be able to look after me. He cannot look after himself.

He cannot even send me an SMS, even though I tried to teach him one whole afternoon. So I have decided to get married in heaven one day, where we will all be the same.

I need dreams, just the way you do. But I adjust my dreams to my abilities.

That was one difficult thing about going to a school with only 'normal' children – you have problems fitting in. So I started to ask the boys whether they wanted my extra chromosome and, because they could not understand what I was saying, they left me alone.

My stepfather tried to teach me to drive, but I am too short. When my feet touch the pedals, I cannot see, and when I sit on cushions, my feet cannot reach the pedals.

I received a Grade 10 certificate before leaving Martie du Plessis High School. In my last year at school, I received a prize for the highest marks in biology and I received the highest honour of the school for drama accomplishments on national level among 'normal' learners.

After leaving school I went to the Motheo College, a technical college, and was also the first and only Down's Syndrome student to be accepted there.

With the grace of our dear Lord, a lot of hard work and an ulcer because I stressed so much, I passed the N3 course, which equals 'matric', and after that I passed the N4, N5 and N6 courses. The N6 course is the highest qualification at the college. I was awarded the Education Diploma in Educare, in May 2009.

When my mother and sister received their degrees, I started to dream about wearing a robe and mortarboard and walking across a podium. When I did eventually walk across a graduation podium all the people in the City Hall stood up for me. I was also awarded a special prize for being the first Down's student to receive a National Diploma. That was the most amazing moment of my life. I looked at all the people and saw my mother and sisters crying.

I am so happy to work at Lettie Fouche, a special school for learners with learning problems, as an assistant in the pre-primary classes. I enjoy every day and I help the teacher to prepare her lessons and to stimulate the learners.

Vanessa Dos Santos of Down's Syndrome South Africa asked me to 'open' the international conference for Down's Syndrome in 2012. She also asked me to be on the International Board for Down's Syndrome.

I live among these people; me, a girl with Down's Syndrome, a condition that makes people abort their babies and lock them in institutions or at the back of their homes so others can't see them!

May you also be blessed with happiness and a heart full of compassion for those in need.

People like this give you hope

Our citizens keep the country together through millions of daily acts of kindness

9 March 2011

My South Africa is the working-class man who called from the airport to return my wallet without a cent missing.

It is the white woman who put all three of her domestic worker's children through the school that her own child attended. It is the politician in one of our rural provinces, Mpumalanga, who returned his salary to the government as a statement that standing with the poor had to be more than words. It is the teacher who worked after school hours every day during the strike to ensure her children did not miss out on learning during the public sector stay-away.

My South Africa is the first-year university student in Bloemfontein who took all the gifts she received for her birthday and donated them, with the permission of the givers, to a home for children in an Aids village. It is the people hurt by racist acts who find it in their hearts to publicly forgive the perpetrators. It is the group of farmers in Paarl who started a top school for the children of farmworkers to ensure they got the best education possible while their parents toiled in the vineyards. It is the farmer's wife in Viljoenskroon who created an education and training centre for the wives of farm labourers so that they could gain the advanced skills required to operate accredited early-learning centres for their own and other children.

My South Africa is that little white boy at a decent school in the Eastern Cape who decided to teach the black boys in the community to play cricket, and to fit them all out with the togs required to play the gentleman's game. It is the two black street children in Durban, caught on camera, who put their spare change into the condensed milk tin of the white beggar. It is the Johannesburg pastor who opened up his church as a place of shelter for illegal immigrants. It is the Afrikaner woman from Boksburg who nailed the white guy who shot and killed one of South Africa's greatest freedom fighters outside his home.

My South Africa is the man who goes to prison for 27 years and comes out embracing his captors, thereby releasing them from their coming misery. It is the activist priest who dives into a crowd of angry people to rescue a woman from a sure necklacing. It is the former police chief who falls to his knees to wash the feet of Mamelodi women whose sons disappeared on his watch; it is the women who forgive him in his act of contrition. It is the Cape Town university psychologist who interviews Prime Evil in Pretoria Central and comes away with emotional attachment, even empathy, for the human being who did such terrible things under apartheid.

My South Africa is the quiet, dignified, determined township mother from Langa, Cape Town, who straightened her back during the years of oppression and decided that her struggle was to raise decent children, insist that they learn, and ensure that they not succumb to bitterness or defeat in the face of overwhelming odds. It is the two young girls who walked 20 km to school every day, even through their matric years, and passed well enough to be accepted into university studies. It is the student who takes on three jobs, during the evenings and at weekends, to find ways of paying for his university studies.

My South Africa is the teenager in a wheelchair who works in townships serving the poor. It is the pastor of a Kenilworth church, where his parishioners were slaughtered, who visits the killers and asks them for forgiveness that he was a beneficiary of apartheid. It is the politician who resigns from her politics on conscientious grounds, giving up status and salary because of objection in principle to a social policy of her political party. It is the young lawyer who decides to dedicate his life to representing those who cannot afford to pay for legal services.

My South Africa is not the angry, corrupt, violent country whose deeds fill the front pages of newspapers and the lead items on the seven o'clock news. It is the South Africa often unseen yet powered by the remarkable lives of ordinary people. It is the citizens who keep the country together through millions of acts of daily kindness.

My South Africa is the people listed in the stories above. They are real. I know them. They give me hope.

Sinoxolo's story of hope

Academic achievement against all odds

24 January 2013

It is, by broad agreement, South Africa's most dangerous school. More than a few pupils at Oscar Mpetha High School in Nyanga, Cape Town, have been wounded or even killed as a result of gang violence in and around the school.

Whenever I visited the school, I was told of yet another break-in and the loss of new computers. Broken windows, dilapidated classrooms and sullen teachers.

This school was the subject of a moving documentary, *Testing Hope*, which followed the lives of a small group of young people through the Grade 12 examinations and into life after school; one young pupil in Molly Blank's documentary was killed in Nyanga before the film was completed.

'Get me out of here,' begged one teacher boasting a rare commerce degree who sat with her peers at the school in a dirty staffroom with tattered textbooks and unmarked scripts all over the place.

I am sure the examiner who wrote to me would be fired if she were tracked down, but this woman changed forever the life of a remarkable young man by sharing his information.

'I don't know the child at all,' says the stranger's email, 'but as a senior marker in history who is once again utterly appalled at the ongoing rampant failure of history pupils at too many schools in the Western Cape, I am amazed at this pupil's remarkable achievement; [we are] intrigued at this outstanding achievement.'

She continues: 'The cognitive skill and articulation required to achieve what I suspect is a mark in the very high 90s in a challenging subject like this would make this pupil a perfect university candidate.'

Now I am seriously intrigued, and what follows is almost impossible.

In the top-ten list from the Western Cape education department you find the familiar list of high achievers from the familiar schools with stretching green lawns, beautiful old buildings, and wealthy parents: Rondebosch Boys, Rhenish Girls, Herzlia, Herschel, Wynberg Girls, Westerford, La Rochelle, Bergvliet and more. But high up in this pack of exceptional schools is the name of Sinoxolo Sem, placed fourth in this illustrious group with an almost perfect score in history.

The name suggests a black pupil, and that does not surprise me at all since the top pupil in history is also not white. What does throw me is the name of the school alongside Sem's surname: Oscar Mpetha High.

After a frantic search, I find his number and call the young man to determine his plans. He has none, especially after a Cape Town university, for reasons impossible to understand, turned him down.

'How would you like to study with us for free?' I ask the young man. The joy in his voice is priceless.

As I write this column in the early morning, we are exchanging text messages on our cell phones as the Greyhound bus hurtles from Cape Town to Bloemfontein. I am about to become the happiest vice chancellor in South Africa.

And so I wish to pay tribute today to the history examiner from Cape Town whose alertness to matters of social justice and inequality will change forever the life of a child who not only survived the mortal dangers of five years inside South Africa's most violent school, but who by some miracle made it to the top of an elite class of schools from the province.

The examiner must know that a first-generation university student who graduates breaks the cycle of poverty in a home; enables siblings to follow in his footsteps with less anxiety; and stands as a role model for others in his school where the horizons of possibility are dimmed by gangster violence and unstable schooling.

She must have felt deeply that such remarkable achievement against the odds must be rewarded, or else the very promise that we hold up to the youth in school will be meaningless.

Then there was another stranger who offered to pay for the bus and my colleagues who offered to put together the money to enable Sem to live in residence, buy books, pay his tuition fees, and have some monthly income for food and clothing. In yet another remarkable way a host of South Africans, who hardly know one another and who never met Sem, from the Cape to Bloemfontein to Johannesburg, pool their meagre resources to make one life possible, a life beyond school.

Whatever you might read elsewhere, I am immensely proud of ordinary South Africans with their extraordinary generosity to look beyond themselves and their own interests by creating life-changing opportunities for promising students without the means to study.

Valley of true visionary

If you despair of the state of education, take a drive to Ntuzuma

7 March 2013

If you feel despair about the state of education in South Africa, take the scenic drive north from Durban's spanking-new airport to an old township called Ntuzuma. After a few tricky turns up and down these characteristically hilly areas you come to the gates of Bonisanani Primary. The high school in the valley below looks like it was burnt out; Bonisanani, by contrast, is surrounded on one side by beautiful patchworks of vegetable gardens grown by the community.

You know there is something different in this school when the rather buxom secretary welcomes you with a firm voice, 'I am in charge here,' and then points to the principal, 'and he knows it!' Chuckles all around.

Bonisanani has the same problems faced by any township school. The hole in the roof reveals the point of entry of the last burglary attempt. The few chairs in the staffroom are withered and torn. Its 90 'orphans and vulnerable children' represent about a fifth of the school's child population.

This school houses a migrant community established for those relocated from three different areas where the Inanda Dam was built. It is tough here, but not for the children – I witnessed the workings of the best primary school I have visited across our vast country.

The tall, handsome, well-dressed principal is in high demand. He was parachuted in a few years ago because of chronic problems at this school. Rumour has it the department is targeting him for another rescue operation. What is it that good principals actually do to turn around their schools?

Nkosinathi Ngubane starts, first of all, with a compelling vision: 'We aim to offer quality education that will produce a disciplined South African who is creative, competent and critical in a secured and child-friendly environment.' I know – you've seen some of this before. Except, this principal actually does quality education.

Second, he looks at familiar problems differently. No water in the school? No problem, he raises funds and installs two JoJo tanks. Too many burglaries? He organises 'night camps' run by parents who catch the thugs – the problem is over. I must say it helps that your chairman of the governing body is a South African Police Service specialist in explosives, and I get the distinct impression that the thieves receive some warming-up exercises before being handed over to the police.

No parental support? Problem fixed with 'door-to-door' orientation sessions for parents. Broken infrastructure? The principal hits the road and brings in funds from the private sector and government departments to build a sports field.

Third, Ngubane recognises that these poor children need a much broader curriculum. So he stuffs his pride in his pocket and approaches the Durban Music School to teach music to the young children. Violins, recorders and clarinets fill the school with music. Bishops, an affluent school in the Cape, is involved in hockey development.

'We copy what is good in other schools,' the unassuming principal says in his PowerPoint presentation.

Through environmental studies, the children tend the gardens and learn hands-on science in the greenery around the school. Sports teams flourish and classrooms are fitted with brightly coloured science and geography materials. Poor children are fed. There is no defeatism here, waiting on government to provide, or holding back children because they are poor and hidden in the hills of Ntuzuma.

The children are sent to compete in maths Olympiads, language festivals and science and technology 'expos', and they win awards. The student elections at this primary school are run by the IEC.

'You can have resources,' the district officer says to us, 'but unless you have a vision to drive the school, the resources mean nothing.' When I read somewhere that a staggering R20 of every R100 of our tax money goes to education, we certainly do not need more money. What we need are school leaders like Ngubane who could turn those resources into results.

'We have no pregnancies in our school,' says the principal, 'because we do virginity testing.' I swallow hard, every progressive bone in my body aching.

The presentation ends with a stirring rendition of Bach's 'If Thou Be Near'. As the notes of the brass quintet float down the hills of Ntuzuma, I mutter to myself: 'Who the hell cares about virginity testing; they got everything else right.'

Seven super numbers

Sorrow was attached to me the way skin lays against the bones

26 January 2012

95, 91, 86, 85, 84, 83, 78. These numbers cannot possibly belong to Valentino Thabang Ndaba, a poor, orphaned girl from Amaoti (10 km inland from Umhlanga), 'the most dangerous place in Durban,' says her supportive mentor, a wonderful humanitarian called Tich Smith.

At the age of five, Valentino's mother died tragically in a car accident, going to her grave with a grand qualification in the family: a diploma in journalism.

In language more befitting an honours student in literature, Valentino writes of that time: 'Sorrow was attached to [me] the way the skin lays against the bones.'

A doting grandmother, together with Lungisani Indlela, a back-to-school organisation, ensured that Valentino became the owner of those unbelievable seven numbers – her Grade 12 results in the 2011 National Senior Certificate.

When I collect Valentino at the Bloemfontein airport, it will be with a knowing joy that she will register to study media and journalism at university.

It did not make sense, two girls running hand-in-hand down a single lane in the 100 m sprint at last week's first-year athletics event. Until I noticed that the one girl was looking the wrong way, to the side and upwards to the heavens.

Now I know, the blind girl running at an astounding pace was Louzanne Coetzee, the only girl who appeared on stage with the group of boys honoured by the minister of basic education when the 2011 NSC results were announced earlier this year. This had never happened before – a blind student racing in the first-year athletics event.

She set a record without knowing it, her life exemplifying determination to do well against all odds.

After I walked arm-in-arm down the aisle with this star matriculant and introduced her to an auditorium packed with first-year parents and our sparkling new students, the audience rose to their feet in thunderous applause for the blind matriculant from a Worcester school.

I was running late for the midnight swim on Tuesday with two first-year residences in the giant university swimming pool on campus. But I needed to print what I had just seen as incoming mail on my Facebook page; this was extraordinary, a completely unexpected message from a science student.

Refiloe wrote:

Prof, I have great news. The botany department is the most integrated department I have ever seen. We had an excursion from January 13 to 20 in the Hogsback mountains, and not once did I feel like we were black and white.

Yesterday, the Afrikaans students asked if we could have class together so now the English and the Afrikaans students have lectures and practicals together.

The lecturers in the botany department are the best and the students are amazing!

What makes an otherwise-ordinary story so moving are the deep fissures that still exist across race, class and language on university campuses, and how students sometimes resolve these issues among themselves and not as a consequence of a policy action.

In this case there is no 'fight-to-the-death' kind of animosity over a language but a resolution of a sticky problem that flows from the forging of friendships in everyday life.

'Did you read today's newspaper?' asked another matriculant from a Cape Town school through a Twitter conversation.

I quickly scanned the online version of the Cape paper, only to find a picture of the youngster floating in thin air after a jump from an aeroplane.

The Little Spirit, Geesie Theron, is the girl with a huge tumour on the brain that had rendered her blind. Despite this, she passed Grade 12 with a bag of distinctions. She had warned me some time back that she was going to jump from a plane.

'Are you serious?' I asked the daring kid from DF Malan High.

'Don't worry,' she retorted, 'I won't know how high it is.'

The nice thing about working in education is bumping into young people every single day who demonstrate what an amazing future this country has as we prepare the next generation of leaders. Here is the antidote to angry, destructive youths who have the same potential for greatness if only we provide the discipline of love and correction.

For more and more children, this will not happen at home, in part because of the growing evidence of single- or no-parent households.

For those who are lucky – a minority like Valentino – significant adults might replace the parents and give hope and counsel.

When the unlucky ones enter school or university, those might be the only places in which they might experience compassion and find direction. If we do this right, expect many more Valentinos, Louzannes, Refiloes and Geesies.

An old-school oasis

This is my kind of school

19 January 2012

Leicester Road School in Kensington has a plaque on the wall honouring the queen and her territories. No, this is not a possession of the Crown in West London; it is a Johannesburg school that is one of the most impressive places of learning I have ever experienced.

It is early Monday morning and, after rising at 4 am for the early flight from Bloemfontein, I was not in the mood for small talk. I expect the teachers on their first day back from the holidays to exhibit that semi-depression that we all go through on returning to hard work.

Exactly the opposite; these teachers are bristling with excitement, almost literally jumping for joy.

'Are you people on uppers?' I ask the one smiling face after the other as they pass by with their joyful countenances.

There are no children yet, but the place is busy. The principal rushes a few to a management meeting. Others read earnestly from what seems like planning books. Nobody is lazing around, and then the shock: one teacher after another comes to tell me how excited they are about teaching and what a great principal they have as leader. This is not choreographed; they really mean it. Time to find out why.

The first thing that strikes you is that nobody talks about academic results. The emphasis at Leicester Road is on caring, and the vision and mission statements on the school website are filled with words of compassion and belonging.

Two teachers tell me with great passion about their love for the children and how hard they work to make every child feel accepted. They raise money to feed hungry children. They employ additional teachers as specialists to guide and counsel troubled children.

The school is basic but clean, efficient and welcoming. The ethic of care is everywhere.

'What is the thing you talk about most on your governance agenda?' I ask the chairwoman of the governing body.

'That the children are okay; that the parents are okay; that the teachers are okay.'

In the cut-throat and competitive focus on academic results, and the threats that teachers and principals are subjected to by the authorities if they do not perform, this school puts care and compassion for their people first. This applies to all.

This is the only school I have visited where the workers also attended my motivational talk and where the staff – teachers and cleaners – appear on one photo in alphabetical order. A small matter, perhaps, but a powerful message that everyone matters on this little oasis in the measurement desert of performance-based education.

Leicester Road is a reminder that we might have gone too far in our obsession with measured results. We might have lost the broader purposes of education to nurture whole human beings with the narrow focus on Annual National Assessments results in primary schools and National Senior Certificate results in high schools.

Of course, children should do better in maths, science and languages, but to what ends?

To prepare calculating automatons for the capitalist workplace, or to produce well-balanced citizens for life in a hurting world?

There is a solid body of research which shows that learning is as much an emotional experience as it is a cognitive process.

Children who are loved and cared for generally do much better with the intellectual demands of the classroom than those who come to school neglected at home and bullied on the playground.

Frightened young people, wondering when a slap from a teacher might come for misspelling a word, or scared of punishment that might follow for under-performing in a maths test, are unlikely to enjoy learning the subject in subsequent years.

Leicester Road restores the humanity that should lie at the heart of education, and is one of the few schools I know that goes against the grain of loveless learning.

As usual, the success of the school lies in its leadership. This is the only school where I am greeted with an almighty hug by the principal and not the formal handshake. Fortunately, black men can't blush.

Renee Abrahams is only the fourth principal in 73 years at Leicester Road and the teachers also tend to form part of a stable personnel tally; after all, who would want to leave this place?

The community around the school has changed as foreigners arrive either as workers or as refugees, but the values of the school remain solid in its embrace of teachers and pupils, workers and parents.

As the teachers begin filing out of the staffroom, the principal reminds them of a borrowed theme to guide them in 2012: 'Dream more, learn more, become more.'

My kind of school.

Beacon for education

You can literally smell a good school

9 February 2012

The bones of the teachers lie buried less than 100 m from the school in a hot, dry corner of the northern Free State. But inside the half-renovated school there is an energy among the living nuns that belies their age and vocation.

A young girl appears at the door of the basic staffroom where we are about to start a short meeting; the child is out of breath and excited, but does not say a word.

The old nun leaps from her seat, grabs the girl's hand, crouches slightly and she sets her sights on the distance, and together they sprint along the brightly polished corridor to where the child wants them to go.

More than 100 years ago, the sisters of Notre Dame made their way from England to this bleak part of central South Africa to minister and later start a school out of which was born St Peter Claver High School.

Here, the children of railway workers and the offspring of destitute parents could receive high-quality education from dedicated teachers, who earned little, if anything, as part of their sacrificial commitments.

The school survived the vicissitudes of 20th-century South Africa, closing and reopening, and withstanding the apartheid legacy.

The site was once handed over to the South African military for training defence force personnel, and reopened again recently.

The nuns came to teach, grew old, and many were buried where they served.

You can literally smell a good school. The fresh paint of the walls, the red polish on the floors, the fresh curtains in the main hall, the neat carpets on the stage, and the immaculately dressed boys and girls.

Coming to the school last week for their reopening, I took a wrong turn into the town with the largest potholes in South Africa.

I saw children from other schools already drifting through town before 11 am.

They looked ragged, aimless, and without any identification, other than various kinds of bags to suggest they might have had school that day. I wave to some of the children, and they return faint smiles in my direction. There's not much to be happy about on this side of town.

'It is not fair,' I say to myself.

How can one group of disadvantaged children in a half-renovated school receive such warm attention and strict pedagogy under the guidance of a group of selfless teachers and yet, less than five minutes away, another group of disadvantaged children is underserved and neglected?

The difference, of course, is not money but values.

At St Peter Claver High you notice two firm values quickly: love and discipline. I notice the way the principal and the teachers talk about the children, how they hold their hands and lift their spirits.

The children are not only loved, they are respected. But I also notice the unwritten rules for behaviour, the ways in which soft discipline is everywhere – from basic but clean, ironed clothing to neat seating patterns, to carefully crafted singing routines. Nothing is out of place. 'This is the way, walk ye in it' – the old scriptures come to mind.

My mind wonders as I await my turn to speak.

What if one could capture those two values of love and discipline in a bottle and transport it across the main road into Maokeng township where the other schools are?

What if the selflessness of the nuns could be injected into teachers from the other schools who would, at the slightest provocation, abandon their duty – the children – in a quest for better salaries?

Of course, educational change is much more complex than my questions allow. But what St Peter Claver reminds you of is that the children on both sides of town are the same children – black, poor, and filled with limitless potential.

How they learn and behave depends on what we as adults do.

How often do I hear teachers try to mislead with these words, 'It is much more difficult to teach today than when you were a teacher', or 'if only the parents would play more of a role', and so on and so on.

Actually, the children are the same from one generation to the next. They respond the same way as children anywhere when faced with those compelling values of love and discipline.

The mind tests me with one more question: What if I could persuade the teachers in the other schools to also agree to be buried where they taught?

Lead from the heart**

The servant-leader is servant first

13 December 2012

Thank you so much for inviting me here to be your guest speaker; it is a great honour.

Wow, I get nervous making a simple speech to my classmates back at school, so please excuse me if I seem to look like a gibbering wreck. Speaking in front of such an esteemed audience like you is something I have never done before.

When Professor Jonathan Jansen invited me to speak, I really thought there was no advice I could give any adult, let alone a whole lot of graduates. But, rather than giving you advice, I will try and explain to you what my campaign has taught me.

My 'Just One Bag' project came about because of a feeling I had in my heart. When it comes to giving or helping, I believe it is 'feeling' that is important; it has to come from within. We can think and devise all sorts of 'nice' things to

** This is an edited version of the graduation speech delivered by Jordan van der Walt at the summer graduation ceremony of the University of the Free State on 6 December 2012. The speech will be circulated to ANC members visiting the campus for their elective conference this weekend. Jordan won the 2012 Inyathelo Award for Philanthropy. His Just One Bag initiative has delivered more than 100 tons of maize to hungry children.

do for people, but if they don't come from the heart, I feel they are meaningless.

You will be going out into this wonderful country of ours to give of your time, help people and serve communities. I believe there is only one way for you to do this properly and that is to do it with your heart.

You have to go out there and want to serve all people because your heart tells you to. If you have become a doctor, or any other professional for that matter, because you think you are going to become rich, drive fancy cars and live in big houses, I think you have made a mistake.

Next year I will go into Grade 7, and my school, St John's, runs a leadership programme which is based on servant leadership. After googling 'servant leadership' I was very interested in some of Robert Greenleaf's work, for it made me think about my campaign and this country. We need leaders in this country, and I am not talking about political leaders – all types of leaders. We are all leaders in some way or other, be it on the sports field, the head of a family or the captain of an industry.

But Greenleaf says: 'The servant-leader is servant first. It begins with the natural feeling that one wants to serve.' And, as I said before – I believe it comes from the heart.

When I was watching that programme about starving children in South Africa, I felt sad. I had a feeling coming from within and I was determined to do something about it. Fortunately, with the help of many people, we have managed to feed over a million people to date. It dawned on me that maybe I am a leader. Yes, I am 12 years old, but because of that feeling of wanting to serve, and a few lifts in my mom's car, I was able to lead. We now have thousands of children who have joined the campaign and it is snowballing.

But, after reading a bit more of Greenleaf's work, I realised what I have started is just that: a start.

Greenleaf asks: 'Do those served grow as persons? Do they, while being served, become healthier, wiser, freer, more autonomous, more likely themselves to become servants? And, what is the effect on the least-privileged in society? Will they benefit or at least not be further deprived?'

What I need to do, is make sure my Just One Bag campaign continues, so those people who are being served will one day in turn serve others as well.

I am sure you have heard of the term '*ubuntu*'. For me, serving is part of *ubuntu* and if we all serve, and we all have *ubuntu*, this country will have no rival.

So my challenge to you wonderful and talented graduates is to go out into South Africa and serve. Do it from the heart because you have a feeling inside you that makes you want to serve. Don't do it for me, don't do it for anyone else – do it for yourself because your heart tells you to.

Thank you so much and I wish you all the best for the future.

Small man made big difference in SA

Nothing in his early life destined Jakes Gerwel for greatness

29 November 2012

He was an unlikely hero. Small in stature, reticent in public, and very soft-spoken, Gert Johannes Gerwel could easily be missed in a crowd. Nothing in his early life destined him for greatness; he grew up on a sheep farm in the rural Eastern Cape in a district of Somerset East.

Yet 'Jakes', as he was called, would become a giant in public life and in higher education.

To a generation of students who sat at his feet, you approached him with caution, for the man had an intimidating grip on politics, society and his first love, Afrikaans literature.

That was precisely why those of us who grew up in the English language were cautious. How could the man find redeeming qualities in Afrikaans? This was, after all, the 1970s and what happened in Soweto had imprinted on young minds an unreflective negativity towards the language of the oppressor.

But the professor could explain the rich and variegated history of Afrikaans better than any, and persuade angry activists of the role of the slaves and the first inhabitants in helping to shape what would have been a more beautiful language had the Nats not messed it up.

Jakes was not, however, a language sentimentalist when it came to Afrikaans. His doctorate (DLitt) at the Free University of Brussels would uncover the misrepresentation of black people in Afrikaans literature, drawing attention to racist stereotypes and the disservice done to the language by white nationalist writers.

It was the way in which he offered a systematic criticism of race and language in literature that impressed, for he was able to keep the attention of conservative white readers even as he wrote in what the target audience then, and some still now, hold to be 'their' language.

What Professor Gerwel will be remembered for in the general population, however, is the boldest act yet of innovation and activism by any university principal – the day he declared the University of the Western Cape to be 'an intellectual home of the left'. Under the sweltering heat of apartheid, he stood up one day and made the most eloquent argument yet for the different traditions embodied in the conservative Afrikaans universities, on the one hand, and the liberal Afrikaans universities, on the other hand. UWC, by contrast, carried a different historical burden and political mission – a place where a critical intellectual tradition rooted in the struggles of the working class would flourish.

In that instance, a struggling 'bush university' started its transformation from an ethnic project of the apartheid state into what has today become one of the most impressive research and teaching universities in South Africa.

That criticality has come to infuse the curriculum, teaching and public events of UWC – something immediately evident to the visitor from outside the Bellville campus.

This is certainly a far cry from the racist professors who taught me; the constant boycotts of classes; and running from tear gas and police during my unpleasant undergraduate student days. The foundations for the transformation of UWC were undoubtedly laid by Gerwel, who held the job of rector between 1986 and 1994.

It came as no surprise that a great honour would fall on Jakes when he was called on to serve as director general in the office of our first president, Nelson Mandela, and cabinet secretary in the government of national unity from 1994 to 1999. With his activist credentials and formidable academic achievements, he could take up academic chairs and leadership positions at universities anywhere in the world; but for him, working in the shadows of our greatest leader, Mandela, meant more than the countless boards on which he served and the string of honorary awards and doctorates he would receive. It is also a measure of his integrity that he did not use that appointment to write about Mandela – a book which would have been a runaway bestseller all over the world given his enormous literary talents.

We seldom spoke; I still treated him as my senior and not somebody you called for purposes of small talk. But at the height of troubles at my current university, Gerwel wrote a moving piece in an Afrikaans newspaper commending our actions and the vision of a future based on healing rather than recrimination. I picked up the phone to thank him not only for that column, but for a life well lived.

Girl's journey from horror to triumph

I always wanted to make a difference in people's lives

1 November 2012

'My father murdered my mother in front of us, my little brother and I; he beat her to death with everything he could find.'

The Grade 12 girl sitting in front of me took some time to complete the sentence as she covered her face with her hands and tears ran through her fingers.

It happened every weekend, the ritual beatings of a mother whom her daughter absolutely adored; the little girl would bear testimony to this brutality and wonder why her mother did not leave. In the harsh life of an informal settlement, her options were limited. When asked whether they wanted their father released from prison where he served time for the murder, the children agreed; they needed the one parent still alive.

Thembi Letsoara (not her real name) was just starting to emerge from an earlier tragedy in which she was brutally raped by her cousin. Nobody would believe her, until days later the doctors would confirm the sexual assault. By this time, the evidence was thin since she had bathed and cleaned up the mess.

The boy's father was the only person working and gave money to the grandmother with whom Thembi was staying; there was an agreement that they would not pursue matters, for that would risk the only source of income available to the extended family.

'For a long time I did not trust male figures, not even my father. I slept with my mother.'

The young woman cries again as she recalls being raped.

Her sole support through this dreadfully painful period of her life was her mother.

'She encouraged me, she loved me, she supported me.'

Now the mother was dead.

It is almost impossible to match this smart, beautiful and well-poised young woman with the two tragedies I had just heard about.

It is even more improbable that her Grade 12 examination results, before these National Senior Certificate finals, include 92% in the mathematics third paper, 94% in the main mathematics paper, and 90% in life sciences.

Having spent only three years, Grades 10 to 12, at one of the top public girls' schools in the country, the young woman overcame poverty, hardship and unspeakable trauma to become a top academic performer.

'She is guaranteed an A aggregate matric,' swears the principal.

Her break came when a famous boys' school invited two children from every disadvantaged school in the area to become part of an academy in which promising learners were given high-quality lessons.

From this large group, two students were sent to that boys' school, and two to the adjacent girls' school. She made it, and took every opportunity to excel not only in academics, but also in senior netball.

There is something I have yet to understand: why most young people, when faced with incredible hardship, give up on life, but a few stand firm and triumph. This thing called resilience fascinates me. Her report card speaks of 'her tenacious spirit' and 'her determination and zealous attitude' and 'going the extra mile to produce work of a high standard'.

But the report also speaks of her humility, her grace, and a 'respectful, quiet and unassuming nature'.

'What is it about you that keeps you going?' I ask.

'My mom, she was my best friend and she was very strong.'

And then she mentions the principal of the academy; this amazing man makes sure that people and the system do not fail her again.

'She wants to study medicine,' the principal tells me, and will need financial assistance and guidance.

'Why medicine?' I ask her.

'Like my mother,' she says, 'I always wanted to make a difference in people's lives. I wanted to make my mother proud.'

It is clear to me that this is not the kind of medical graduate who will jet off to Europe after a state-subsidised education. She will plough back right here.

'If your mother were here, what would you say to her?'

She does not need to think.

'I would say thank you for raising me, for supporting me, for believing in me.'

And then my final question: 'What is the one thing you would want your mother to know about you today?'

With a soft, confident voice: 'I am now stronger than I have ever been.'

Imam who shook SA***

Don't let him have died in vain

4 October 2012

Two events of seismic proportions shook the Western Cape in the closing days of September 1969. The first was the Ceres-Tulbagh earthquake of 29 September which registered 6.3 on the Richter scale. The aftershocks continued until 14 April 1970, and the effects of the quake were felt more than 1 000 km away in Durban.

The second seismic shock was the murder on the night of 27 September in the Maitland police cells of the 44-year-old Imam of the Stegman Street Mosque, Abdulla Haron, the editor of *Moslem News*; the husband of Galiema; and the father of three young children – Shamila, Mogamet and Fatima.

That death – the 12th political prisoner to die in police custody between 1963 and 1969 – sent forth tremors of grief and protest that registered shock waves well beyond the borders of South Africa.

That we are gathered here this evening for the Fifth Annual Imam Haron Memorial Lecture bears witness to the fact that we have not forgotten that political earthquake that marked the death of such a courageous leader.

*** *Speech delivered on the occasion of the Fifth Annual Imam Abdullah Haron Memorial Lecture, 2 October 2012, Salt River.*

I congratulate the organisers for ensuring that every generation of young South Africans learns the lessons of faith and courage given to us through the life of Imam Haron, for we need to be reminded of the price that was paid for our freedom, and why we dare not tolerate what passes for education and decency in our country.

I was 13 when the lesser quake hit the Western Cape; my parents would tease me for years afterwards that I slept through my birthday night (29 September), blissfully unaware of the commotion on the streets of Retreat where we lived.

What I did not sleep through, in the manner of speaking, was the other earthquake, for throughout my teenage years I was reminded – at school and university and in the community – of the imam who 'accidentally fell down the stairs' and died, even though the alleged fall could not, according to the inquest, account for all 27 blue-green bruises on the body.

Since that time, we mocked the official versions of activists who died in detention as a result of slipping on a bar of soap, or jumping from a window, or hanging themselves or falling down stairs.

There are several qualities of Imam Haron that struck me as worth sharing.

- His strong sense of humane values rooted in his faith. He expressed a strong commitment to the values of freedom, dignity, respect and fairness, and this came through clearly and repeatedly in his rousing public addresses.

- His deep commitment to education. Even though he did not have the opportunity to proceed beyond primary schooling, he was passionate about education for his children and others.
- His passion for a better society. He had within his vision a society that was not based on racism and discrimination but equality for all human beings, including freedom of worship – something he stood on strongly when it came to the immovable position of mosques under the Group Areas Act.
- His courage in the face of injustice. There was a growing awareness that the dragnet of the apartheid system was closing in on him, and that he should have made plans to escape the country a long time ago. But he stood his ground.
- His internationalist orientation to the understanding of society. He travelled widely at a time when few did, and gradually developed a fine-tuned understanding of global struggles for justice and the solidarity of those in north Africa and Europe.
- His non-partisan perspective with respect to others. While he was a devout Muslim, he also served people in Langa, Gugulethu and Nyanga. He consolidated Muslim–Christian relations from his base in Athlone.

What made Imam Haron such a threat to the apartheid state was his refusal to separate school and society; education and community; faith and activism; individual agency and political authority. To him, it was the same thing.

If we all make this commitment, then Imam Abdulla Haron would not have died in vain. In fact, he would still be with us through his powerful, enduring legacy. In that sense Mary Elizabeth Frye might well have been speaking of Imam Haron in the closing words of her wonderful poem 'Do Not Stand at My Grave and Weep':

Do not stand at my grave and cry,

I am not there, I did not die.

Bona fide progressive leaves a lasting legacy

He was the standard for a revolutionary

30 August 2012

I knew only one genuine revolutionary in my life, and he died this week. The news floored me, and for an hour I roamed around the office in a daze.

'It is not true,' I kept telling myself, for this great man, simply by being present in our country, kept alive my dreams and hopes of what a real revolutionary was and could be.

'Neville just died,' said a mutual friend on Monday morning, and an era ended right there.

Dr Neville Edward Alexander seldom spoke of the hard years on Robben Island, so I was delighted to collect this (edited) snippet from former Archbishop and fellow islander Njongonkulu Ndungane on Facebook this week:

One of the episodes I remember vividly was the arrival of Alexander's group on Robben Island. [Their] reputation preceded them. Warders leapt forward with great alacrity saying: 'Waar is daardie Neville Alexander?' Out came this diminutive, skinny person. The warders' response? 'Jy lieg [You lie].'

They then took a well-built member of his team by the scruff of the neck and sent him packing to the isolation cells. Consequently, we had a whole month sitting at the feet of the master.

There is a more durable story here about a man who was different in every way from what his standing as a scholar and his reputation as an activist suggested.

He was fearless in the struggle and fearsome in the articulation of his ideals for a socialist Azania. Yet this same comrade worked with everyone 'from communists to whale lovers', as a close friend of his put it, in his non-partisan, tireless struggle for education.

On the one hand, he fought against racism on the part of the Afrikaner nationalists and their prejudicial attempts at ethnic ownership of the Afrikaans language; yet Alexander was one of the most persistent activists who argued for Afrikaans as an effective medium for mother-tongue learning and a potential vehicle for reconciliation.

What made comrade Alexander so obviously different from the nouveau riche – as he sometimes referred to the new elite and their unearned wealth – was his simple life-style when he could so easily have cashed in on his prized PhD from Tübingen, Germany, and his enviable credentials as a struggle hero. But he did not, determined to remain below the radar when fellow prisoners basked in the limelight of media attention, some elevated to god-like status even by those who once imprisoned them.

Alexander was different, and for a long time he did not drive a car or own a cell phone. He lived until his death in a shared home in a depressed area of the Cape Flats called Lotus River, where even light rains could cause water to overflow 'the avenues'. He dressed simply and lived modestly. Even his famous book carried an unflashy title, *An Ordinary Country*.

At our first meeting he invited me to sit on the floor and enjoy lunch, which was fish and chips wrapped inside the pages of a newspaper, in a modest house doubling as a non-governmental organisation.

His most telling critique of South African society was the four-nation thesis and the dangers of 'fighting race with race'. Perhaps because he lived in two race-obsessed countries, Germany and South Africa, he knew, better than most, how our obsession with racial categories in the distribution of resources would surely come back to haunt us. You could, in fact, issue no greater insult to this great humanitarian than to call him 'coloured'.

He was a thorn in the flesh of his colleagues at the University of Cape Town with their antiquated attachment to race and ethnicity as the basis for making decisions on admissions to medical school.

Every few months Alexander would call me and a few friends to discuss the deep crisis in school education. We would talk for hours about the social upheaval that would befall this country if the injustice of unequal education continued. But then he acted on his concerns, taking teams of language specialists into the townships of Cape Town and demonstrating how mother-tongue instruction and multilingualism could improve the educational outcomes of children and bring young people out of poverty.

He was a thinker and a doer. He was an activist who did not wait for the government to wake up to the enormity of the education crisis.

When I hear uncouth youth leaders and older politicians throwing around words like 'revolutionary' and 'counter-revolutionary', I know those are political games. After all, I knew the standard for a revolutionary: Dr Neville Edward Alexander.

Seftel science for all

We need to change the way we talk about science

22 March 2012

When Harry Seftel talks about a bladder infection on television, you wish you had one.

What this former Wits medical science professor has achieved in his discipline is to communicate a medical problem to ordinary citizens in a way that makes sense and that even generates excitement about the condition. Most scientists lack this important skill – to communicate the elegance, beauty and inspiration of their science to non-experts in ways that convey insight and fire the imagination.

Scientists are trained to communicate with their peers at highbrow conferences and in atmospheric journals. The language is necessarily complex and arcane, but that is acceptable for the normally small community of scientists working in that narrow field. But scientists increasingly have a broader responsibility: to educate and inform the public about science, scientific discovery and the meanings of scientific wisdom in everyday life.

The same applies to professionals. We still have too many doctors in this country who treat patients as 'things'. I have often had to interrupt a doctor to ask what exactly is wrong with me. Why are you giving me this kind of medicine? What side effects, if any, could I expect to have?

When the mildly irritated doctor begins to answer, it is with words that, had I not had some elementary training in human biology, I would have no idea what he was trying to say. In part this reticence to communicate about your body is a habit of history; doctors were all-knowing demigods who simply had to prescribe a medicine and you, the patient, were only too grateful to be granted an audience with His Worship.

But scientists also have a broader responsibility to educate because the immediate problems of climate change or mad cow disease or cholera or HIV/Aids demand that we communicate clearly and simply with ordinary citizens, who are all affected by these potentially harmful conditions. Rather than treat the public as passive subjects to be informed on a need-to-know basis, we need to shift our training of scientists to make public understanding and communication of science a curricular requirement and a professional habit.

The catastrophic consequences of a previous government policy casting doubt on the link between HIV and Aids could have been mitigated by scientists courageous and competent to communicate a simple health message to millions of the most vulnerable South Africans at the time.

There is another reason why such simple communication is critical in a nation that on paper assigns high importance to science and technology as important areas of investment and development. One major obstacle in the way of such ambition is the low levels of scientific literacy in the school population.

The foundations of science learning in South African primary schools are weak, even if measured narrowly in terms of both national and international tests of achievement; that we already know. The small numbers of students taking physical science at high school, and the low levels of achievement in Grade 12, are widely known.

One reason for this state of affairs is the way in which science is taught in most of our schools. Science is taught formally, often outside the world of application. Physics equations are memorised without meaning. Student misconceptions are corrected as errors rather than as inevitable even among scientists as insight develops. Science as an examination subject has meant that teachers often trawl through old examination papers, having long given up on the notion of science learning as fun or science as foundational to many inspiring careers.

This could change if the public communication of science was much more pervasive in urban and rural schools throughout South Africa. There are, of course, some state-sponsored science events held once a year and even some science magazines distributed to schools. But for science to become part of our everyday experience, it has to be much more commonplace in all kinds of media: in inter-school competitions; in radio call-in quiz games; and in popular magazines and the like.

The biggest challenge for teachers is learning how to turn formal science into everyday science. Few training institutions offer this kind of insight. It requires teachers who not only know a lot of formal science but can 'see' such science in everyday operations. For example, ask a science teacher why a commercial airline travelling from Johannesburg to New York has to stop for fuel along the way, but a plane coming from the Big Apple back to Joey's does not, and you will find out how uncommon is everyday knowledge of science.

We need to clone Harry Seftel.

Reaching new horizons

When is it appropriate to close a school?

16 August 2012

When is it appropriate to close a school? Forget for a moment the childish, opportunistic politics of rival parties in the Western Cape.

You close a school when the number of pupils is very small and you cannot justify the overall costs of keeping it open.

You shut down a school when a number of under-enrolled schools exist in the same area; combining pupils in one full school makes more financial sense.

But there is another, more controversial reason to close a school: when it experiences chronic failure and no interventions can turn around its outcomes.

Based on visits to thousands of schools over the years, I wish to venture that about 15% to 20% of our public schools are so deeply dysfunctional that nothing can be done to rescue the children damned for a lifetime by sitting inside those cold, uncaring buildings (if these exist) where teaching and learning were supposed to take place.

As my car went slipping and sliding dangerously through the snow on the icy roads of the eastern Free State last week, I called ahead to suggest to the principal that he close the high school where I was scheduled to speak to a huge hall filled with pupils. He was reluctant to do so because New Horizon College had planned this event for months and, as I was to find out, they had invited several other high schools from the Harrismith area. So they sent home by bus only those children from rural QwaQwa, fearing that the roads towards the Maluti mountains would probably be closed by the time the event was done.

I am glad they did not close the whole school because what I was about to witness bears powerful testimony to what can happen when thousands of children from failing public schools are transferred to an independent community school.

At New Horizon College nobody fails Grade 12. For five years in a row they have obtained 100% passes. This all-black school remains among the top schools in the province and places pupils among the top performers in the region.

After five minutes on the property, you know why. The discipline is firm; every poor child is immaculately dressed in uniform.

The rich extra-curricular programme takes pupils to entrepreneurial competitions in New York and to national science and mathematics competitions.

The quality of drama and singing is among the best I have seen in privileged schools. The language skills and sophistication of the pupils are of a standard I've seldom seen at the best universities. And the motivational levels of the pupils are simply awe-inspiring.

Same children – different school environment.

A high-quality private school for township children was the brainchild of the ageing Vernon Botha, a man who clocked years of service in the education of the disadvantaged. Why could he and his team succeed where the regular government schools did not?

To start, they choose their own teachers, a diverse team of professionals led by a caring, competent and conscientious principal.

The capacity to hire highly competent and motivated teachers is lost on ordinary public schools where race, ethnicity, political-party affiliation and family connections are among the factors that get the wrong teachers appointed. And then the most innovative of schemes anywhere: 'All parents automatically become part of the school governing body upon enrolling their child.'

What a brilliant idea to ensure parental involvement, and accountability, in the life of the school.

I watched the children from the surrounding public schools also gathered in the school hall of New Horizon College. They looked sad and downcast. Their uniforms were not the same. Their responses to the interactive session lacked energy and enthusiasm. My heart breaks. These are the same children, only in different schools.

It is time to consider closing more government schools and, gulp, turning them over to the independent sector.

We can respond ideologically to this proposal, and I can give my usual speech about the merits of public education from which my own children also benefited.

But they went to good public schools; the majority of our children do not. All I know is year after year we fail tens of thousands of pupils in the vain hope that teachers will take them seriously, that learning materials will arrive on time, and that test scores begin to reflect the real potential of our children.

An oasis of love, care

A school where hurt meets healing

24 May 2012

If you've started to lose hope in the education of the poor, you must find your way to a little gem of a school at the bottom-end of a dead-end street in the once-infamous Point area near the Durban harbour.

I was responding to a warm letter of invitation to surprise the soon-to-be-retired principal of the school, a joyful character called Gail Theunissen. When I stepped through her door in the early morning, the headmistress looked stunned, then ran around her desk to cry with joy on the shoulder of the visitor.

What followed was a whirlwind tour of some classrooms, a corridor meeting with some of the teachers, and a stunning concert by these young children of Addington Primary School.

You can sense a happy school, and this was it. But there is hardship here, a place of hunger and hope, a school where hurt meets healing.

Here is the face of South Africa's future inner-city school of 1 500 pupils: more than 300 children from other African countries. Mainly black children.

The few white children, I am told, come from poor families, some of whom live in shelters. Every slice of South African society is present.

I meet a respected young Zimbabwean teacher in this multifaith school. The children at Addington Primary have one thing in common: hardship.

'I do not like these photographs,' says the principal, 'I just want to take them all down.'

I am curious as she waves away the ageing wall photographs.

'Because it does not represent us.'

The old photos of all-white children remind the visitor of a bygone era in this school of 117 years; the middle-class whites have fled in part, I suspect, because of the social decay around the school before the area again became prime property with the building of the magnificent uShaka Marine World next to Addington Primary.

What makes this school different is that Theunissen and her strong management team and core of outstanding teachers kept the academic culture of the school intact.

The decline into poverty did not mean a decline in educational standards, and that is highly unusual in the country's transition.

The rich and growing diversity of the staff by colour and creed has, in fact, elevated the standards of the school – standards of academic excellence matched with standards of human compassion.

Every class is humming with activity, every child is known in person. Given the severe hunger experienced by some pupils, there is also a school nutrition programme.

The education department gives very little to this excellent school to maintain its basic but neat facilities, so outside sponsors have to be sought to give these precious children a decent standard of education.

So what keeps this school together despite the common fate of so many schools where a change of class invariably means a slide in academic standards? It is the leadership of principal Theunissen.

As I watch her perform her duties, she satisfies the seven qualities of good school leaders in tough school environments.

One, she believes in distributed leadership: sharing leadership and authority across the team of school managers.

Two, she spells out a clear and simple vision for the school (pasted on the wall) behind which she rallies every citizen inside those walls.

Three, she combines a strong academic culture inside the classroom with a supportive extra-curricular programme outside the classroom.

Four, she tells every child how good they are and what they can become.

Five, she lifts the spirit of the school by being present, physically and emotionally, as she celebrates the work of her teachers and her children in public.

Six, she maintains an attractive physical environment in the classroom and on the playground, recognising that children's attitudes towards life and learning are dependent on their sense of care in the immediate surroundings.

Seven, she has created an inclusive environment in which people from different race, class, ethnic, religious and national diversities are recognised and appreciated.

'A man has three goats and four sheep,' I quiz the Grade 3 class before I leave. 'How many dogs does he have?' They jump into frenzied intellectual activity to try to solve the problem using various mathematical combinations of three and four. Who cares whether they get the right answer; they are learning, they are loved, and they are excelling inside a promising school.

EPILOGUE

Embracing the enemy – put yourself in the shoes of the man working to have Nelson Mandela killed

27 June 2013

'This is treason par excellence!' shrieks the former debt collector, the son of Lithuanian immigrant Jews, in his closing prosecutorial statement in the Treason Trial of Mandela and eight others. Sabotage means a jail sentence; treason gets you hanged.

Judge Quartus de Wet agrees that the charges represent 'in essence treason', but hands down the lesser sentence. Mandela escapes the hangman's noose, leaving us with an awful 'what if' question: what if he had been hanged?

Percy Yutar must have been a miserable man when the country's first democratic president invited him to lunch. They talk for about an hour and the former prosecutor calls the 'terrorist' he was trying to hang 'a saintly man'. Yutar dies at 90, trying to rebuild his reputation by arguing that he made the case for sabotage since Mandela and his comrades did not deserve to hang.

Put yourself in the shoes of the wife of apartheid's intellectual architect, who secludes herself in a dusty, dry, whites-only enclave in the Northern Cape called Orania.

Until the day she dies, Betsie Verwoerd will carry the burden of a name that continues to be a swear word in black South Africa. She, too, is invited to tea with the president, but declines, citing ill health. She makes the mistake of saying, if the president is in her area, he would be welcome to visit.

To the surprise of all, he does, and spends 45 minutes over coffee with the ailing old woman who offered him 'pure Afrikaner hospitality', the visitor recalls.

She dies a Verwoerd aged 98, an unrepentant separatist whose community welcome made Mandela feel 'as if I was in Soweto'.

Put yourself in the shoes of the man who spent 22 of Mandela's 27 years in prison with him, much of them scouring the prisoner's incoming and outgoing mail. The ever-courteous Mandela says nice things about this 'polished and soft-spoken' man until Warrant Officer James Gregory senses opportunity and writes a book – actually, it is written for him by a tabloid newspaper in the UK – called *Goodbye Bafana*. Even fellow prison warders dismiss the book as replete with lies and exaggeration – for example, he did not spend leisurely hours with Madiba talking politics or foil an assassination attempt on the famous prisoner.

Yet Gregory is invited, with two other prison guards – Christo Brand and Jack Swart – to the inauguration of President Mandela, even after having disgraced himself by publicising intimate and often untrue accounts of their life together. What should have been a badge of shame, being Mandela's jailor, he tries to turn into personal and commercial benefit.

Gregory dies of cancer at 62 having changed his mind about 'the terrorist' he later called 'the perfect gentleman'. Was Mandela's great legacy of reconciliation merely an example of his political savvy, a careful calculation meant to ease racial tensions in a country that was very much at war with itself even after his release from three prisons – Robben Island, Pollsmoor, Victor Verster – in succession?

Or was there something much deeper to the man and his motivations in reaching out to three troubled souls who found themselves on the wrong side of one of the 20th century's greatest tragedies – apartheid?

The answer to these important questions is found in a powerful paragraph on the prison warders from *Long Walk to Freedom* that gives a rare insight into the deeper emotions and convictions of Mandela about human beings: 'Men like Swart, Gregory and Warrant Officer Brand reinforced my belief in the essential humanity, even of those who had kept me behind bars for the previous twenty-seven and a half years.'

In other words, when Mandela looked at Yutar, Verwoerd or Gregory, he did something the rest of us (still) fail to grasp. He looked past their official roles – their perpetrator status, individual weaknesses and dangerous ignorance. He looked through the façade of appearance and performance; he saw and reached out to that 'essential humanity' that made them like the rest of us.

In doing so, he not only offered the individuals a chance at redemption, he offered a whole country a model for reconciliation.

Put yourself in the shoes of Mandela. We all now need to start our own long walk to freedom, learning from this colossus who gave us our humanity back.

Rather than this undignified spectacle of panic and performance by mourners and opportunists alike, we need to reflect quietly on what Madiba tried to teach us in his own special way.